MASTERING THE ART OF MEDIA MESSAGING

MICHAEL S. EMERSON

OVERLORD PRESS

LOS ANGELES

Manufactured in the United States of America.

Overlord Press
Los Angeles, California

ISBN 978-0-615-90854-0

*I dedicate this book with deep appreciation to my children,
wife, extended family, loved ones, friends and colleagues, who
throughout the years, have endured my obsession with the
Media and its influences on the day-to-day lives
of each and every one of us.*

Those who can, lead; those who can't, criticize!

Anonymous

CONTENTS

FOREWORD

Congratulations! You are about to learn the secrets that Media professionals *don't* want you to know.

Contained within the pages of this book is an insider's look at the driving forces behind—and the influential techniques used—to dominate the story selection and reporting of America's news, entertainment and information-oriented medias.

Furthermore, once you've learned these secrets, I'll provide you with tried and tested, step by step techniques teaching you how to:

- Ensure Reporters treat you and your story, fairly and accurately, each time and every time.
- Dominate press interviews and control news conferences.
- Package your message(s) in a Media friendly and effective manner.
- Place yourself, your company and/or your product(s) on national media—and do it for free!

And that's just a sampling of what's awaiting you!

American Media is the most powerful molder of ideas and marketer of products ever conceived. The secret to using it successfully is first, knowing how it works, and then making it work for you!

Mastering the Art of Media Messaging will show you how to accomplish exactly that!

INTRODUCTION

If you're expecting a book full of wordy, long-winded explanations that first provides you with the information you need and then proceeds to restate that same information in three different ways for the single purpose of adding pages to their dissertation, then this isn't the book for you.

I have too much respect for both your intelligence and your time to do that.

Mastering the Art of Media Messaging will provide you with a wealth of concise information, materials, formulas and examples to effectively identify and then utilize the most powerful communication, information and motivational tool ever conceived by Man.

In 21st Century America, Media has evolved as a commanding influence permeating every aspect of our waking world.

It has the power to topple Presidents, neutralize armies, and create or destroy billion dollar corporations.

By definition, Media is a process through which any organized, mass dissemination of information is conveyed. Such would include all forms of print media (newspapers, magazines, periodicals etc.) as well as the electronic media, specifically, radio, television, feature films and the Internet, etc.

However, it's the purpose of this survivor's guide to provide decision makers with the insights they need to effectively, efficiently, openly, honestly and authoritatively interact with the one form of Media that affects America, (especially corporate America) the most: the news media.

Media is not the enemy; it's a tool, and this guide will teach how to put that tool to good use.

Michael S. Emerson
Los Angeles

MASTERING THE ART OF MEDIA MESSAGING

Chapter One
MEDIA'S HIDDEN SECRETS

In 1963, at the age of 16, I attended a communications seminar held at the then Ambassador Hotel in Los Angeles. It was the pre-cable TV era and the attendees were discussing the revolution in communications awaiting our futures.

However, what I remember most about that conference was a banner that stretched from one end of the ballroom the other. It read: *Mass Media Molds the Minds of Modern Man.*

Truer words have never been written.

We live in a different world than our forefathers. Super Sonic transports speed our travel, computers speed our thoughts, and media permeates every aspect of our lives.

It never ceases to amaze me though, how individuals who have overcome the impossible by successfully building multi-million dollar industries, or managing multi-national companies or creating multi-billion dollar global markets, stand frozen in fear at the prospect of being confronted by the news media. However, those fears are not without some foundation.

Recently, I had breakfast with the CEO of one of America's top Fortune 500 companies. He was frustrated because an interview he had given was reported inaccurately. The facts used weren't false, but they weren't true either. The Reporter had chosen to use half-truths in order to taint and titillate the information the executive had provided to paint the short term prospects of his company in a negative fashion. The resulting article caused the company's stock values to suffer resulting in an over night loss of literally tens of millions of dollars to the company's stockholders.

Sadly, this is not uncommon. Recently, a false internet rumor caused the stock of a major airline to free-fall from thirteen dollars a share to below three dollars a share within a four hour period. The stock recovered once the rumor was proven inaccurate, but in the meantime thousands of stockholders had lost millions of dollars in the resulting panic. (As a side note, before breakfast was over, I taught that CEO a two-step program he can use to ensure that mistake never happens again. You'll find that technique explained, in detail, in Chapter Five, *Awakening the Dragon Slayer).*

Granted, media can be intimidating, but remember, the best defense against intimidation is education!

To understand what makes media so influential in today's society, you must first understand *Media's Three Principles of Power.*

Media's First Principle of Power
THE MONEY MACHINE

This realization is more than just an insight, it's an epiphany!

Once you understand that Money (and desire for more of it) is the greatest, single driving force behind all forms of media, you then have the tools needed to harness that power and make media work *for* you instead of *against* you!

In many of my speeches and lectures I ask my audiences this question: *What is the purpose of Media? Is it to educate? To entertain? To inform?*

It is very rare anyone ever answers this question correctly.

The purpose of media—its *sole* purpose—is to make money!

You may ask, *But what about Public Broadcasting or non-profit organizations that sponsor media oriented materials?* Trust me! Every major media entity is driven by money. Take PBS. Its goal is to provide enough programming of interest to persuade their viewers to send them what? MONEY! It's the same with all the non-profit organizations that provided a variety of media oriented materials such as newspapers, magazines, radio and television programming. Every one of them is constantly driving to justify their jobs or their existence in exchange for monetary rewards. And frankly, that's the way it should be!

Here's an irony for you. While Media publicly prides itself on its adversarial activism against corporate America, very few of this country's corporations come close in size, power and *profitability* to America's Media giants, and none of them can equal Media's ability to influence America, her people and her way of life! (Remember, *Mass Media Molds the Minds of Modern Man.*)

Being driven by the quest for money, in and of itself, is not a bad thing. I think it's a good thing! Where the media gets into trouble is when they begin to compromise integrity and truth in their pursuit of fame and fortune.

In the game of Media, ratings represent the audience and the audience represents revenues.

Always remember, two time-proven, key ingredients used by the News Media to capture those audiences they so desperately seek are negativity and controversy!

Consequently, if you ever find yourself on the wrong end of a media covered—or created—controversy, sadly, more often then not, *your* truth and *your* facts are secondary to *their* story. It is your image and your presentation which the media will respond to—and report on!

When faced with that situation, in Chapter Six: *The Rules of Engagement,* you'll find specific steps you can take to ensure that your corporate image and your media message is presented in the most authoritative and positive manner possible, the first time and every time.

Media's Second Principle of Power
THE IMPRIMATUR OF IMPORTANCE

Without debate, one of media's greatest elements of influence is its ability to decide, almost without challenge, what *is* and what *is not* important to our 21st Century culture.

Let that simple fact sink in!

When the media focuses its attention on a story, then the public's perception is *that story must be important or they wouldn't report it.*

Conversely, if media chooses to ignore or downplay a story, event, issue or accomplishment, then the public's perception is that it must not be important and thus not worthy of the public's admiration, concern, or attention.

Imagine the power you would hold, it you alone could decide what was important in this world and what wasn't.

Whether you realize it or not, in fact and in practice, that is *exactly* what Media does!

Through common practices such as story placement and the intensity of coverage with which a story is reported, Media first tells us *what* we should be thinking about and second, what we should be *thinking* about it!

Media further emphasizes this point through a variety of reporting techniques, the two most notable of which are story grouping and story association.

Story Grouping refers to the positioning (i.e. placement) of the story in the overall news report. If it runs in the beginning half of the news program (or above the fold in the newspaper) then the story is given a higher degree of urgency or importance than if it is allowed to run in the program's second half (or in the below the fold).

Story Association is a little less obvious, but can be even more damaging.

It usually takes one of two forms: the first is the grouping of your story with similar stories of either a negative or positive nature. For example, if it is your intent to get coverage for a new product line you're about to release and your story is preceded by a positive Dow Jones report, your story will benefit from being associated with that positive news.

If, however, your new product line follows a negative business report (i.e. corporate mismanagement, investor fraud, etc) then your report will be tainted by the negative nature of the preceding story.

The second form of association is unspoken. It is the graphic that appears in corner of the screen over the report's shoulder. If it's a positive picture or complimentary image of you, your company or your products, it will only serve to affirm the report.

If however, say you're a pharmaceutical company releasing a new line of cancer treatments and the graphic depicts a medical symbol with dollar signs over it, your story's connotation would have a negative impact on its audiences, even though the report itself could be either positive or neutral in nature. (Chapter Six, *The Rules of Engagement*, outlines the specific steps you can take to minimize the potential for negative association in the reporting of your story, self or company.)

Story Association can also apply to the individuals reporting the story as well. For instance, if your local station or favorite network has an on-air personality most closely identified with the uncovering of consumer fraud schemes, any service, product or personality he or she reports on is then immediately suspect.

Conversely, prior to his untimely death in 2005, ABC network anchor Peter Jennings hosted a series of television programs entitled, *UFOs: Seeing Is Believing*. The mere fact Mr. Jennings lent himself to those programs, gave a new and immediate sense of credibility and respectability to a subject matter many deemed lacking those two key elements.

Media's Third Principle of Power
THE PHENOMENON OF IMPLIED AUTHORITY

Ask yourself these two simple questions:

1. *Can Media really influence the way American's think and act?* If you answer *yes* (and you should), then ask yourself

2. *From where, then, does media derive its power to influence modern societies?* The answer is *the societies themselves!*

We *watch,* we *listen,* and sometimes we even *react,* but rarely do we ever *challenge* Media's impact on our lives!

Not only do we *give* media the power to influence us, but the majority of us give it willingly, openly and completely!

In a freedom loving society, we willingly delegate to others authority over us in exchange for a responsible and responsive system of checks and balances, (i.e. the Constitutional right to life, liberty and the pursuit of happiness), empowered by individual rights, responsibilities and legal recourses.

However, once you enter the arena of Media, all that changes.

Be careful not to misunderstand what I am saying. A responsive, free, open, balanced and responsible press is essential to the strength and survival of an open democracy and a free market.

The operative words however, are *free, open, balanced* and *responsible.*

When television came into its own in the late forties, audiences nationwide were mesmerized when their living rooms played host to a cavalcade of world newsmakers and Hollywood celebrities.

One of the casualties of television's success however, was that over the next two decades, news programming (i.e. the organized mass dissemination of factual information) was slowly transformed from "the act of reporting" into "the art of entertainment". Why? Because of their drive to improve ratings or more specifically, *their need to improve revenues,* i.e. the empirical exercise of *Media's First Principle of Power.*

Another of Media's most self-empowering attributes contributing to its implied authority is its ability to control its own rebuttal.

When Media makes a mistake and reports a false or factually inaccurate story, how is the public to know about it unless the Media themselves broadcast their own failures?

Remember, *Media's Second Principle of Power.* It they don't acknowledge it, it must not be important!

Consequently, the only medium with the reach, impact and authority to hold Media accountable is the Media itself!

This is such an important insight; allow me to repeat it one more time: *The only medium with the reach, impact and "authority" to hold Media accountable is the Media itself!* More on this point later.

Chapter Three, *Show Me the Power,* will provide you a step-by-step method to use this simple, yet highly effective, little known and less used fact to level the playing field of American Public Opinion.

That's not to say Media should be feared—far from it! Media is not the enemy: Media is a tool! Not just any tool. But the most powerful, informational and motivational tool ever conceived by mankind!

However, as with all forms of effective technologies, those using the Media (or being used by it) need an operations manual in order to:

1. Ensure that you're using Media and all the tools it offers efficiently and effectively, and

2. To make sure you're not damaged by it in the process.

Mastering the Art of Media Messaging is that manual!

Chapter Two
ME, MYSELF and I

Here's a twist.

When I was 11 years old, I knew that when I grew up I wanted to do one of two things: either serve in the Priesthood or work in Media. When you think about it, they're related. Both are people oriented careers, both designed to serve the community and both are perceived as authority figures, whether deserved or not.

At 13, I entered Our Lady Queen of Angeles Junior Seminary and realized in a relatively short period of time that maybe the Priesthood wasn't my calling. At that time, there was actually a waiting list of young men wanting to enter the Seminary, so I did the honorable thing and relinquished my spot for someone more inclined for a higher calling.

I transferred to Beverly Hills High School and ended up graduating with such future notables as actor Richard Dreyfuss; actor and director Rob Reiner and actor and comedian Albert Brooks (whose given name is actually Albert Einstein—true!).

It was the mid sixties and the Vietnam War was just starting to heat-up.

ME, THE MILITARY AND THE MEDIA

As with many of my friends, upon entering college, I joined the Army Reserve for a six-year enlistment as a weekend warrior. Little did I know my experiences there would change the course of my life.

Within a few years of joining, then President Nixon ended the draft, so all branches of the services began advertising themselves to the public in hopes of seeking volunteer recruits.

Out of the blue, one weekend, my commanding officer ordered me to take a recruiting unit to a neighborhood shopping center in hopes of signing new enlistments. That day, we were successful in recruiting five individuals. To my surprise, all five failed the mental test and yet all five men were eventually enlisted in the United States Army Reserve (sad, but true).

Call me Patriotic, but that incident had a deeply negative affect on me. (I should mention here that my college degrees are in the fields of Marketing and Advertising, not Media nor Communications. Everything I have learned about how Media works, why it works and how to make it work for you has been learned over a period of 35 years plus in the Studio not in the classroom!)

When our Reserve Unit met the following month, I approached my commanding officer and expressed my concern over the caliber of recruits we were attracting. I suggested a new approach: Television.

He gave me the green light and on my own time, I perfected a method of getting myself booked as a guest on local media (both television and radio) to discuss the benefits of serving in the United States Army Reserve, of which there are many.

Through a long series of trial and errors, I quickly learned what makes Media tick and have continued to use that knowledge repeatedly and successfully over the past three decades.

Within a few months, my appearances on a variety of talk and issued-oriented television and radio programs exceeded everyone's expectations, especially my own.

I still remember the statistics. After one of my typical on-air appearances to discuss the benefits and controversies surrounding the Army Reserves (remember, by this time, the Vietnam War was in full force), every time I gave out a recruitment phone number, that phone line would be jammed for an average of three days!

ME, THE MILITARY AND MADISON AVENUE

Before long, news of my successes made its way to Washington, D.C. and I was ordered, by no less than the Secretary of the Army himself, to report to the Pentagon to explain my successful media methods to all those interested.

Picture this: I'm all of 26 years old and I'm sitting in a board room at the Pentagon surrounded by Madison Avenue executives from the advertising agency N.W. Ayer &

Son on one side and a room full of brass (generals and full colonels) on the other.

The ad executives were openly defiant and clearly cynical at best. I didn't blame them. After all, they were being paid millions of tax dollars to buy television and radio ad time promoting the Reserves and here was this kid from California who was getting far better results and my air time was for *free*.

More importantly, *the phone inquiries from my appearances exceeded the paid ads by a factor of fifteen-to-one!*

As for myself however, I didn't consider the situation an adversarial one. I was there to explain what I did and how I did it. I naively thought the ad execs would welcome my ideas and then train others around the country to use them as effectively as I was.

As I said, I was young.

Things turned a little ugly in the meeting when the Madison Avenue executives claimed my successes were a fluke and couldn't be replicated on a regular basis.

With that, all eyes turned to me and in my youth and arrogance, I thought for half a second and then responded, "If you truly believe that, then *you* pick two cities in the country where you think my system won't work, and I'll prove to you it will."

The men from Madison Avenue jumped at the challenge but reserved the right to research the cities prior to choosing them. We all agreed and I caught the next flight home to California.

Two weeks later, I received a phone call from OCAR (Office of the Chief of Army Reserve) giving me my assignment. The cities the Ad Executives selected were Seattle, Washington and Milwaukee, Wisconsin.

Research had shown it had been over five years since any pro-military PSA's (Public Service Announcements) had aired in either of those markets. Again, remember a large portion of public opinion—especially in Seattle—was firmly against America's involvement in the war.

It was then and there that I decided Seattle would be my first target.

Within three days after arriving in Seattle, I appeared on two television shows, three radio shows and taped three PSA's for delayed airings (each of which was produced and paid for by the individual station airing them).

My trip was a huge success and Milwaukee was to be equally receptive.

I had proven my system worked. Never again did I ever meet my Madison Avenue comrades, but it was decided I would be reassigned from Sixth Army (which is based in California) to OCAR (Office of Chief of Army Reserve) at The Pentagon so they could send me on Media excursions anywhere in the country without worrying about local Military Command jurisdictional issues.

Over the next several years, for two days a month, I'd journey to my assigned cities and booked myself on the appropriate radio and television programs to promote the benefits of serving within the Army Reserve.

Prior to my discharge from the military, the Pentagon presented me with a plaque signifying that my media methods had successfully generated in excess of 1.5 million dollars (that's in 1975 dollars) in free and highly-effective advertising time for the United States Army Reserve. I still have that plaque.

In Chapter Nine, *Leader of the Pack,* I explain, in detail, the seven techniques you can use to get yourself booked as a guest on television and radio programs all over America, *and to do it for free!*

FACE TO FACE

As mentioned, although my degrees are in Advertising and Marketing, I have spent the last 35 plus years of my life as a member of the working media. Mt career began in 1979, when I embarked on a broadcast career by creating and hosting the radio news feature *Face to Face.* Although the program began airing on only 18 stations, within twelve months it had grown to 126 stations within the US and 697 stations in 41 nations around the world.

Face to Face was a five day a week, five minute, news-oriented, radio feature consisting of two minutes of commercials and three minutes of content (interviews) with world known personalities.

My guests on *Face to Face* were literally the world's Who's Who of Politics, Business and Entertainment. Guests such as then Secretary of State Henry Kissinger, Prime Ministers Margaret Thatcher of Britain and Meacham Begin of

Israel and King Faud of Saudi Arabia along with Bob Hope, David Rockefeller and The Archbishop of Canterbury. I'm sure you get the point.

While hosting *Face to Face*, I maintained press credentials with the White House, The Senate and The US House of Representatives.

My routine would take me to Washington D.C., about once every three weeks. After checking into my hotel, I'd head to the White House Press Room to catch up with who was in town and what events were scheduled.

The procedure was always the same. First, I'd call ahead to say I was coming. Then I'd report to the northwest gate of the White House, be cleared and begin my walk up that winding path from the gate to the West Wing where the Oval office and the Press Room are located. I made that walk dozens of times and yet, each and every time I did, the same thought would enter my mind. "Who the hell are you to be walking into the White House?" I'd always answer myself the same way "You're nobody, but you host a radio program that is heard all over the world. It's your audience that's important, not you."

I hosted *Face to Face* for four years and over 1,400 broadcasts, but left for the opportunity to work in television.

I miss the spontaneity of radio and the opportunities my audience gave me to meet daily, one on one, with the world's newsmakers. However, for the last three decades

I've made a very comfortable living as a writer, director and producer of film and television programming.

Either way, Media is my life, and I love it!

Chapter Three
SHOW ME THE POWER!

I confess.

People fascinate me. I love watching them in airports, train stations, shopping centers etc: anywhere and everywhere that people are going about their daily lives. I love to speculate about what they do, where they're going or from whence they came. But the people who fascinate me the most are those corporate leaders, both men and women, who think nothing of taking on Wall Street; pushing the edge of the marketing envelope, forging new technological, financial and/or record-breaking frontiers while competing toe-to-toe with their world's competitors. But when it comes to Media, they seem to perceive it as an eight hundred pound gorilla asleep in the corner. Their greatest hope is that it won't awaken, and most importantly, won't awaken and come after them!

That's their single, greatest mistake! Instead of hoping that gorilla won't notice them, they should pick up a 2 by 4 piece of wood, walk up to it and hit it squarely over the head, and when it awakens, make it dance to their tune!

And here's how to accomplish exactly that that!

We've already discussed how the driving force behind all forms of Media is profit, but what about the men and women who run Media? Those individuals, whose job is to decide what's important enough to be reported and how it should be reported, what are the driving forces behind them?

Is it Influence? Power? Money? You guessed it, it's all three!

Remember this formula; **(AA) x (AR) = R**. I'll explain it in a moment.

The majority of people who work in Media love doing the work they do. I know because I'm one of them. For the most part, the work is interesting, financially rewarding and most importantly, ego stroking!

The human drive to succeed, to be rewarded for your efforts and respected by your peers is not only normal, but highly desirable.

However, since few occupations have the power and impact Media has on people, their lives, and their pocketbooks, I think the rest of America needs an "equalizer" to help battle Media Goliath, so here it is!

The formula (**AA**) x (**AR**) = **R** stands for **A**udience **A**ppeal (i.e. Influence) times **A**udience **R**each (i.e. Power) = **R**emuneration (i.e. Money).

Once upon a time in a land far, far away, those news people (in both the electronic and printed press) whose hard work and dedication earned them the public's respect and recognition were referred to by management as "Star Reporters." Now they're referred to as "Talent" or "Media Personalities."

That says it all.

Today, a reporter or media personality is considered successful when he or she has reached celebrity status. It doesn't matter what the medium—radio, television or print—once they're known and respected by their audience, their job is secure, their career is solid and their income is substantial, i.e. they have achieved their influence, which leads to them obtaining power and , in turn, money.

Two such individuals who are the living examples of the of the (AA) + (AR) = R formula are radio personality Rush Limbaugh whose audience appeal earns him a reported fifty million dollars a year, and TODAY Show host Matt Lauer who, although was earning a reported seventeen million dollars a year in 2012, demanded a pay increase to a reported twenty-five million dollars a year in 2013, and got it!

The genesis of this achievement however, is the phrase, *respected by their audiences.*

POWER VERSUS VULNERABILITY

There is a very interesting thing about power: it's always balanced by vulnerability. The bigger they are, the harder they fall.

A reporter can be beautiful or handsome, charming, intelligent, articulate, athletic and dynamic, but unless they command one key element, it's all for not. That element is credibility.

Once a news network loses its credibility, it loses its audience. However, once a reporter or media personality loses credibility, they lose their job! And it is there that the playing field of public opinion is most level.

A learned man once said, *every story has two sides, only the truth has but one!*

Remember, fiction may be more entertaining, it may even be more believable, but the truth is always more powerful.

Audiences may prefer reading fiction, but when it comes to the news, they expect the truth.

Accuracy and accountability—these are your greatest equalizers.

Challenge a reporter's credibility and you threaten the single, greatest element through which they exist.

Yet, before doing so, first ask yourself, when is such a challenge appropriate? and most importantly, how can a challenge questioning a reporter's credibility be substantiated?

Keep reading.

Chapter Four
MY TRILOGIES OF TRUTH

When I was a very young man, my father instilled in me the reality, *it's not how much money you <u>make</u>, it's how much money you <u>keep</u> that counts.*

The same holds true for messaging.

When it comes to the Media, more often than naught, how you *present* your message has more of an impact on your audience than the actual *contents* of your message.

Because today's Media is such a fast paced, entertainment driven, audio and visual spectrum, you, your company and your message must be ready to "step up to the bat" using those same criteria.

Therefore, to assist you in packaging and presenting your message in an effective and impressive manner, I have created a three step program entitled my *Trilogies of Truth* to ensure your issues are properly constructed, delivered and received the first time and every time!

My First Trilogy of Truth
IMAGE EQUALS PERCEPTION

The attitude and image you project speaks volumes about the message you're attempting to convey.

Allow me to state that again: *The attitude and image you project speaks volumes about the message you're attempting to convey.*

If you project an attitude of self-confidence, it will be perceived as knowledge and authority.

Conversely, if you project an attitude of hesitation or doubt it will be perceived by your audience as weakness, insincerity or even worse, misrepresentation.

Your appearance is even more important!

That's because your image is the first word your audience hears and the last word they remember. If you doubt that, just ask any prominent criminal attorney. What's the first thing they do before they present their client to a prospective jury? They give them a complete make-over starting with how they look and how they dress. Why? Because they know how they present their clients (i.e. how the jury *perceives* their clients) can and often does make the difference a verdict of guilt or innocence.

Here's a real life example of the right message but the wrong image.

Following the 2004 California Gubernatorial election, I was having dinner with William Simon, the Republican candidate who tried unsuccessfully to unseat the then sitting governor, Gray Davis. (Ten months after winning that election, Governor Davis was recalled by the voters of California and Arnold Schwarzenegger was elected governor).

During dinner I turned to Bill and said, "Your campaign must have had the best media advice money could buy and you chose to ignore every bit of it; or, you must have had the worse possible advice and followed every syllable of it!"

He replied, "It was the latter." Allow me to demonstrate.

In one of his political ads, Bill was seen walking in the surf along what seemed to be the Malibu coastline; as I remember, he was barefoot and wearing trousers with the cuffs rolled up. He delivered a pro-environmental message at the end of which he walked up the sand and joined his wife and children who were standing next to a rather large beach house.

Now there is no doubt in my mind that Bill is a committed environmentalist who cares deeply about our environment and the effects it has on not only our generation, but generations yet unborn. However, in this case, although his message may have been correct, the *image* was all wrong!

Mistake Number One:

Bill comes from a very distinguished and successful corporate and political family, a fact that worked against him in the campaign. The *last* thing he needed was to look like some corporate CEO trying to fit in with the common man at the beach by wearing his long pants with the rolled up bottoms while walking barefoot in the water.

Mistake Number Two:

There is nothing wrong with having Bill's family join him in the shot (after all, they are all very attractive and intelligent looking individuals, a definite plus to any campaign). The problem arose *where* he met them—specifically, standing next to a large beach house—the impression being it was *his* multi-million dollar Malibu beachfront house!

In my opinion, it didn't matter what Bill was saying in his political ad, the *message* that came across visually was *another rich republican trying to fake it and come across as just an ordinary guy spending a day at the beach . . . as he stood outside his multi-million dollar Malibu beach home!* Not exactly a message to which the ordinary voter could relate! In the end, the ad came off as insincere at best! Not only was the ad a total waste of time and money, but in my opinion, it *hurt* his image more than helped it.

That same political message could have handled in a number of effective and positive ways, for instance:

Option One:

If Bill wanted to show his family in the commercial, he could have had his children playing in the ocean, all of whom would look very natural in a beach environment. Then he and his wife, both dressed in appropriate beach attire, could have discussed how important the environment is to all of us and what he would do as Governor to protect it. That would have been a far more natural, thus more believable message.

Option Two:

However, had I been asked, I would have suggested he go in a totally different direction. Remember, the intent of the political spot was to convey to California's electorate Bill's strong commitment to environmental issues.

I would have solicited the help of a true credentialed environmentalist; found those common grounds in which he (or she) agreed with Bill's vision and then I would have the environmentalist appear on the beach, without Bill nor his family, discussing the importance of the environment to all of us and then add, *"Bill Simon agrees with me, and that's why I'm voting for him for Governor!"*

In essence, the appearance of a noted environmentalist would have given other like-minded Californians *permission* for them to vote for Bill Simon. (For more on the influence of "granting permission," refer to my *Seventh Commandment of Communication* listed in Chapter 8).

I believe that message would have been far more credible; much more appealing and thus, more effective!

It's true, believe *in your message and your audience will believe in you.* But if you fail to present your message in a believable manner, your efforts could (and most often does) have the exact opposite affect on your targeted audiences. I see it everyday in ads coming out of Madison Avenue; very expensive ads whose intent is to help bolster the image of their clients and their products, when in reality, through poor writing and imagery, they have the exact opposite affect.

A more recent example can be found in the 2010, California Senatorial campaign of Republican, Carly Fiorina.

Carly is a retired executive of Hewett Packard who was hoping to unseat a multi-termed Democrat Senator named Barbara Boxer. It is not my intent, nor desire to dissect the pros and cons of Fiorina's political strategies, but I will focus on one huge weakness that was prevalent throughout her entire campaign; specifically, how her campaign spots projected her image as a leader, a woman, a wife and a mother.

I do not know nor have I ever met Carly Fiorina, but I do have several friends who do know her and the one thing they all agree upon is how warm, caring and outwardly friendly she is.

That fact was lost in every one of her campaign commercials.

In every commercial I saw, when she appeared she was filmed in a medium or "3 Button Shot" (so named because the camera frames the person with the third button of their shirt or blouse positioned at the bottom of the frame). She was placed in front of a background which was not flattering to her features nor her skin color and with lighting that made her look hard and withdrawn.

Had I been asked (and I wasn't), I would have had her filmed listening to the concerns of others; smiling and interacting with young and old alike and capturing the positive results her warmth and caring personality was having on others.

Her opponent had painted her as a ruthless and heartless businesswoman and unfortunately, at least in my opinion, Carly's own commercials seemed to confirm that accusation.

Carly Fiorina allowed her opponent to define her image; and that image ended up defining the voting public's perception of *who* she was and *what* she wasn't!

Never allow your adversaries or competition to define how the public's perceives who you are and for what you stand.

My Second Trilogy of Truth
PERCEPTION IS REALITY!

Ralph Waldo Emerson wrote: *"When the eyes say one thing and the tongue another, the practiced person relies on the language of the first."*

Simply stated, what Ralph was saying was *what people perceive is what people believe.*

It's the nature of being human: Our perceptions are our realities.

How others see us, is how they perceive us to be!

This reality should be a key guideline in selecting the individuals who will represent your image, your philosophy and your positions to the news media.

Case in point:

In flipping through the television channels, I am always amazed at the reality program *Cops*. More specifically, I am dumfounded at whom some police chiefs select to represent their department (and thus their city) to the media world.

Here is how it works. Generally speaking, the producers approach (or are approached by) various police departments throughout the country asking them if they would like to participate in the making of the television program. If they agree, the chief then assigns some of his officers with whom a *Cops* video crew will ride for their shift.

So far, so good.

In my mind, where the mistake is made is when the officer (or deputy sheriff) selected to appear on this nationally syndicated program is so physically challenged (i.e. overweight) that he (or she) has difficulty getting in and out of their cruiser, much less chasing down a suspect.

As a result of that image, what is the nation's perception of the effectiveness and efficiency of that city's police department?

Given the opportunity to shine in front of the entire nation, I would hope that a chief of police would take the time to select an officer (man or woman) who is ascetically pleasing, energetic, articulate and athletically fit to represent the rank and file of his (or her) department—and their city! But far too often, that's not the case.

We can all learn a lesson from *Cops*.

As superficial as it may sound, reality dictates, that the individual selected to represent you, your organization and your beliefs often times, can, and will have, more of a major impact on how your image or message is received and perceived than the message itself!

The individual selected to represent your company or philosophy to the Media, (i.e. the PIO (Public Information Officer) or other media representatives) should possess at least five of the six following attributes:

1. An articulate individual with the ability to think on his or her feet.

2. Should be pleasing to the eye; well groomed and physically fit.

3. Have a command knowledge of the products, services, history, and situation to which they are addressing.

4. They should project a professional attitude and positive personality.

5. Radiate an image of energy and confidence, and,

6. When possible, be proficient in more than one language.

Always remember, Media is a world of images and sound bites.

Sometimes the simplest things may be hard for us to recognize and even harder to understand, but in the world of media you need to live by the following truisms:

1. Simplicity is King;

2. The image you project is the reality by which you will be perceived, and

3. How you are perceived sets the rules as to how you will be treated.

My Third Trilogy of Truth
WORDS ARE POWER

For millennium, the power of the pen has been both praised and criticized but *always* utilized in the ongoing war of ideas!

It may be an old cliché, but that doesn't make the statement any less factual. Simply stated, Words mean something!

Remember that fact and then choose your words wisely because the words you choose *will* make or break your message. Just ask *Fox News!*

When the Fox News Network was created, they chose to identify themselves with two simple words, words when taken individually have little impact, but when used together, especially in conjunction with a news organization, cut to the very core of credibility and believability. Those words: Fair and Balanced!

The impact of those two words on the viewing public (together with their commitment to provide their audiences with a view of the news overlooked by their competitors) helped catapult *Fox News* to the number one watched cable news network in America.

The simple phrase, "Fair and Balanced" was so effective, a rival news organization sued *Fox News* and asked a court to forbid them the right to use those words in the promotion of their news programming. The case was thrown out of court and today, when the majority of the American public hears the phrase "Fair and Balanced," they think of *Fox News!*

Another case in point:

There was a time in my life where, for three years, I lived in a cozy (another word for small) waterfront apartment located in a Southern California Marina. It was a three story apartment building with twenty apartments on each floor; with each of the apartments facing out onto the boat-filled marina and the blue Pacific beyond.

Over the years, I had become friendly with the man who owned the apartment complex. He openly discussed with his tenants his intention to convert his apartment building into individual waterfront condominiums and sell them for hundreds of thousands dollars apiece.

As that day approached and his apartment conversion finally received the city's blessing, I ran into Michael (the building's owner) coming out of the Club House. As I saw him, a thought entered my mind and the following conversation occurred.

I stopped Michael and asked, if I could show him a way to add an additional one hundred thousand dollars to his bottom line net profit, without adding any additional costs to his conversion, would he let me live there rent-free for the next several months until the conversion was complete and the condos were put up for sale?

He thought for a moment and asked, "I put an additional $100,000 in my pocket with no additional expense to me?"

I answered in the affirmative.

"And in turn, you get to live here rent free for the next four to six months?" he asked.

Again, I answered in the affirmative.

He grinned widely and said, "Deal!" and put out his hand to shake on it.

As mentioned, the apartment building was three stories high, with twenty apartments on each floor. The first floor apartments (soon to be condominiums) were numbered 101, 102, 103, etc. The second floor apartments were numbered 201, 202, 203, etc. as was the third floor at 301, 302, 303, etc.

I explained to Michael, that all he had to do was to change the numbering of the third floor units from 301, 302, 303 to Penthouse 1, Penthouse 2, Penthouse 3, etc. and then add $5,000 to the purchase price to each of the third floor units because now the buyers of those units would no longer be the owners of a Marina "Condo," they would now be the owner of a Marina "Penthouse."

It took only a moment for him to digest my proposal and then he smiled, shook my hand for a second time and said, "Congratulations, you are now living here rent-free!"

Words mean something and to my former landlord, one word, "Penthouse," meant an additional $100,000 in profits.

As demonstrated, words are all powerful. They pacify, excite, inform, motivate, and decimate both our intellects and emotions.

While in college pursuing a degree in Advertising, I was continually amazed how words and their simplicity of use could almost guarantee a predictable reaction from the buying public.

Ask yourself, what are the two most used and most effective words in the world of advertising? The answer: *new* and *improved* !

Think about it. Those two words have inspired consumers to try, retry, and then retry again, again, and again a wide variety of products in hopes of discovering better cleaning agents, brighter detergents, tastier sauces, and healthier foods. Even if you've already tried and discarded those very same products because of their failure to live up to your expectations, if they're now "new and improved," they're probably worth a second, third, fourth, or fifth chance to win you over.

Words are powerful tools, so choose them carefully and use them well.

Chapter Five
AWAKENING THE DRAGON SLAYER

The term *dragon* is generally defined as "a mythical creature, typically reptilian in nature and possessing magical qualities."

Media is far from being mythical as it is *very* real, and the people who represent it certainly cannot be termed visually "reptilian in nature," especially since the majority of them are selected for their appearance rather than their aptitudes. But the two things that Media *does* have in common with dragons are its seemingly magical powers, and its terrifying qualities.

Before proceeding much further, I need to reiterate: *Never be intimidated by Media*—it's simply another tool to be used in your business!

More importantly, it is a tool with seemingly magical powers capable of informing, motivating, enlightening, inspiring and persuading the human psyche as no other tool that's come before it.

Then the million dollar question is, how can we put that tool to work *for* us instead of having others put it to work *against* us?

The following are some simple, yet highly affective methods to accomplish exactly that! Let's start with the easiest solutions and work our way up.

TAKING CONTROL OF THE INTERVIEW

In Chapter One, I referenced a breakfast meeting I had with the CEOs of one of America's Fortune 500 corporations. A few days earlier, he had participated in an interview with a newspaper reporter discussing a variety of topics concerning the scope and direction of his company's goals and objectives. When the reporter's article appeared in the paper, it was less than complimentary. The resulting fallout was a negative impact on the company's stock and the loss of millions of dollars to his stockholders.

He was not a happy CEO.

I asked him if the information reported was inaccurate. His answer: *yes and no.* It seemed the reporter had used half truths and implied facts upon which to base his negativity towards my friend's company.

I felt for him because it is a story I have heard far too often. Consequently, I suggested he use the following interviewing techniques to ensure that it would never happen to him again.

STEP ONE:

The next time he was to be interviewed by a reporter, I suggested, just prior to the start of the interview, that he have his secretary walk in *and place a tape recorder on the table between him and the interviewer and then press the recording button!*

I then suggested he start the interview with the phrase, *I hope you don't mind, but I want a transcription of this interview for my records.*

Think about the impact that one simple, decisive action has on your interviewer. In that one, single action, you have leveled the playing field.

Until that moment, the reporter was holding all the cards. Because the *only* record of what was being said during that interview was in his (or her) hands!

As soon as that recorder was placed on the table and the record button pushed, all that changed and the power and dynamics of the discourse shifted in the favor of a more fair and balanced interview.

In a non-threatening manner, the reporter was instantly put on notice that they would now be held accountable for the truth and accuracy of the facts upon which the article would be based.

Not only would the recorder be capturing the questions and answers of the interview, but it would also be recording the vocal inflections, insinuations and attitude of the interviewer!

This procedure holds true for all forms of media-related interviews. When you are being interviewed for a newspaper article or for a radio interview, a simple voice-activated recorder will work wonders in helping to ensure the fairness and accuracy of the information reported.

If you are scheduled for a television interview, make sure you have your own cameras right there along side of the news crew's cameras.

I recommend always using two cameras, even if the news reporter is only using one. Why? Because, the first camera should always be focused on the person being interviewed. Having the interview documented on video tape will not only help ensure factual accuracy, but it can also serve a valuable tool in helping to train both you and your executives on how to look and act on camera.

However, I strongly recommend you have a second camera and use it to focus entirely on the interviewer.

I promise you, it is a reality that won't be lost on them!

Ninety-five percent of the time, you will find them being on their very best behavior and bending over backwards to ensure a fair and factual report.

But what those five percent who don't?

THE GUARANTEED SOLUTION
STEP TWO:

This is a biggie, but you will never have to do this more than once or twice in your lifetime because it is guaranteed to send a shock wave throughout the news media; putting everyone on notice that when it comes to you and your company, you expect and will settle for nothing less than accuracy and factual professionalism.

Remember: *This only works if you have been wronged and that wrong can be documented.*

Let's surmise that your interview has gone well and the contents of which have been captured either on audio or video tape.

The article or report appears and it is full of inaccuracies and false conclusions. What do you do? The old way of dealing with these issues was to ignore them because to correct them would only draw more attention to the falsehoods and open yourself up to further reporting inaccuracies.

In the reality of today's world, that is exactly what *not* to do!

In the twenty-first century, nothing ever goes away! The internet sees to that! Furthermore, any unchallenged misinformation will quickly become documented facts.

Here's the guaranteed solution.

A) **If the article appeared in a print media:**

1. Go directly to the publication in which the inaccurate report appeared. (If the article was a syndicated one, select one of the largest media outlets in which it ran).

2. Prepare a full page display advertisement stating your case clearly and succinctly. I suggest you use an interest grabbing headline such as, *Judge for Yourself.*

3. Specify the date the article appeared and most importantly, make sure the reporter's name is *prominently* mentioned throughout your ad. If a useable photo of the reporter is available, all the better.

4. State the facts then reference how they had been compromised or distorted by the reporter's misreporting. This is most effectively accomplished by quoting, verbatim, from the transcripts of your interview, then quoting from the reporter's article and then asking the reader to *judge for yourself* as to the accuracy of his (or her) reporting.

5. Finally, encourage the reader to visit your corporate website to either read or *listen* to the interview in its entirety.

B) **If the report was via radio or television:**

1. Contact the broadcast entity and make arrangements to purchase a series of thirty second commercial spots. (I recommend from 6 to 9 spots. My reasoning for recommending 6 to 9 spots is to allow for morning, noon and evening coverage for a minimum of two to three broadcast days).

2. If radio, purchase the spots during their news breaks for morning drive time; the noontime news and the afternoon drive time as these usually represent the heaviest listened air times.

If television, you'll only need to purchase three spots to be run during their news broadcasts. Just make sure at least one of those spots is run during their nightly news reports.

3. Following the techniques I've outlined under *Perception is Reality!* (Chapter Four), through a professionally

produced spot, have a media savvy representative present your case in a concise and authoritative manner while repeatedly referencing the reporter by name. Start by sparking the curiosity of the viewers as to the nature of the controversy and then urge them to visit your website to read the actual transcripts of the interview and compare those facts with the ones presented in the aired report. Then urge them to *judge for yourself* as to the factual accuracy of the reporting. During your spot, emphasize the importance of responsible news reporting in a free society and the absolute importance of accuracy and credibility in the reporting of that news.

4. Finally, it is always extremely effective to include a sound bite within the body of your spot to support your argument. Something such as *Although every story may have two sides, we believe the truth has but one!*

You may be saying to yourself, *But this will cost a fortune!* The simple fact of the matter is that it won't, but doing nothing will!

For example, there is no need to run any national ads, all you need is local coverage *provided you run it in the city where the reporter in question works.* (Another way to minimize your costs of production is to investigate your local cable outlets and find out which companies they recommend to produce the commercials they are running for their clients).

The image you want to project is one of professionalism and sincerity so make sure your commercial is professionally written, acted (or Voiced-Over) and sweet-ened (music and audio tracks mixed properly).

Here's the heart of this exercise.

If you think I am recommending these steps in order to correct the misinformation reported about you, your company, product, services and positions, you need to go back and re-read Chapter Three, *Show Me the Power*.

In it you will find the single greatest *power* a reporter has is his or her credibility, but it is also their greatest w*eakness*.

In this simple action, you have called in to question that reporter's judgment, ethics, fairness and biasness. In other words, you have used the very medium from which they derive their power and influence (Media) to challenge their reporting credentials!

The result will be immediate, widespread and long-lasting.

Immediately, expect to be challenged by the reporter in question and his immediate supervisor. This is a good thing provided you are prepared to back up your claims of unprofessional actions and misreporting by utilizing your copy of the recorded interview.

What you won't see is the incredible, immediate and long term impact your actions will have on every other journalist within your reporting community. That's because one of Media's dirty little secrets is reporters don't write for the public; they write for each other! Too often they care what their fellow reporters think of their work more than the accuracy of their facts. The very last thing any of them want is to have *their* name singled out and to have *their* ethics and capabilities challenged within the arena of public opinion.

Consequently, the next time (and every time thereafter) you or any of your people are interviewed (and a recording of that interview is taped by you) you can rest assured that the resulting article or news report will be a thorough, balanced and accurate one.

THE KISSINGER METHOD

You need to realize the news media is used to working in a faceless, pack mentality. Consequently, while in that environment, it is not unusual for them to compromise thoroughness and accuracy for laziness, sensationalism and expediency.

But single them out from that pack and lure them into the light of day and for the most part, you will find them to be both polite and professional.

I have learned this fact, first hand, from one of the best media handlers of the 20th Century, Dr. Henry Kissinger.

It was in the early years of the Carter Administration. Henry Kissinger had recently left public service after serving as both United States Secretary of State and National Security Advisor to both Presidents Richard Nixon and Gerald Ford.

I had interviewed him at The Biltmore Hotel in Santa Barbara, California, for my internationally syndicated radio news feature *Face to Face.*

Following our interview, he invited me to stay for a scheduled news conference with both the local and national news media.

I hope I can adequately paint this picture for you.

I entered the back of a large auditorium where at least 250 news reporters had gathered. Moments later, a door opens and Dr. Kissinger entered the stage from the right. As he made his way to the center podium, the press corps erupted in a series of loud questions being repeatedly shouted at the former United States Secretary of State and Presidential National Security Advisor, in a disrespectful manner.

The yelling was almost deafening.

As soon as Dr. Kissinger reached the podium he raised his hands to quiet the shouting media. Within moments, a hush fell across the room.

In his very distinctive voice, Dr. Kissinger began his press conference by saying the following: *Ladies and gentlemen, I promise that I will answer every one of your questions to the best of my ability under the following three conditions. First, that you raise you hands and wait until I call on you. Second, when I do call on you, please stand, and third, that you then clearly state your name and the news organization you represent.*

I will never, ever forget what happened next. It was as if a light had been turned on in the room and everyone was suddenly on their very best behavior. No more shouting, no more lack of respect.

Simply stated, Dr. Kissinger had separated each of them from the pack, identified the organizations they represented and then addressed them as individuals. In return, each individual responded professionally and respectfully.

Approximately a year later, I was interviewing the CEO of one of the world's largest corporations for my program *Face to Face.*

Because I feel it appropriate to protect his identity, let it suffice to say his company had been in the national headlines under some rather unfavorable conditions.

I had interviewed him in his suite at a downtown hotel in Los Angeles. I felt our interview had been respectful yet, incisive and evidentially, so did he.

When wrapping up our recording equipment, he approached me, thanked me for my professionalism and then added, "I doubt if the press mob waiting for me down stairs will be as professional as you."

I laughed, then told him my story about Kissinger and suggested he follow the master's example and set the same three ground rules going in.

Less than a week later, I received a handwritten note on his personal stationery stating simply, "Michael, it worked! I owe you one."

He had entered a room full of aggressive, dead-line driven reporters and transformed them in to a professionally conducted press conference.

True story.

Here is another true story concerning a multi-national oil conglomerate, which while in the midst of a media-crisis, effectively use some of the same tools outlined in this book to make the media work for them while the news media itself were doing everything they could to work *against* them!

On April 20, 2010, the Gulf of Mexico's deep water ocean drilling rig, *Deepwater Horizon,* then licensed to the energy conglomerate British Petroleum, suffered a catastrophic explosion resulting in the death of eleven workers and making it the most watched, most reported on oil spin in history.

On April 23, 2010, the United States Coast Guard deployed remote underwater cameras showing the escaping crude oil and reported that the wellhead was leaking 1,000 barrels of crude oil per day (bpd). (Five days later, the USCG revised its estimate upward to 5,000 bpd, but before the story was over, estimates varied from 20,000 to 100,000 bpd. However most experts now agree the flow ranged from 20,000 to 40,000 bpd.)

As previously stated, I am using this real life example of an environmental accident being turned into a media-hyped catastrophic event because I believe it is an excellent example on how to make media work *for* you instead of *against* you!

In the days immediately following the blow-out, (specifically April 23rd) The USCG together with The Homeland Security Agency reported, "The incident poses a negligible risk to regional oil supply markets and will not cause significant national economic impacts."

That same day, the Obama administration's press secretary Robert Gibbs said, "I doubt this is the first accident that has happened and I doubt if it will be the last."

So far, so good. A legitimate news story has been reported on in a responsible way, but all that is about to change.

The most potentially explosive (i.e. dangerous) types of news stories are those driven by images. Especially if those images fail to tell the whole story!

Remember that remote camera place at the leaking well head by The United States Coast Guard to monitor the leakage? Well those images of black crude being spilled into the blue waters of the Gulf Coast had now captured both national and international attention.

Those images were now driving the story, not the facts! (You may recall, in *Media's First Principle of Power*, it is stated that *if you ever find yourself on the wrong end of a media covered or media created controversy, sadly, more often then not, your truth and your facts are secondary to their story. It is your image and your presentation which the media will respond to—and report on!*

It is not my intent to minimize the effects of the spill, nor to make excuses for the mistakes made which led up to it. However, it is my intent to applaud BP and its then Chairman Tony Hayward for their effective use of Media to help manage a runaway news event (rather than story) which, by now was being driven by emotion and politics (a deadly combination) rather than facts and realities.

The first correct (and courageous) thing Tony Hayward did was to make himself available to the news media on a regular and plentiful basis in order to answer all their questions in an informative and apparently, sincere and meaningful manner.

Next, he repeatedly announced that BP was accepting responsibility for the spill and all legitimate claims would be paid in an expedient manner. (This simple action diffused a potentially a totally separate emotional and potentially explosive storyline.)

Realizing that at the time, the United States was experiencing severe unemployment, and that the oil spill would only add to that suffering, Hayward also announced that BP would be hiring local residents to assist in the massive cleanup already underway. Again, the right move at the right time.

But this next step was his most brilliant. The chairman of BP announced that his company was spending 20 million dollars on public service announcements—advertising—in order to keep the public informed as to their progress and ongoing efforts to right this wrong. In addition, they would also create commercials promoting tourism to the Gulf in hope of minimizing the spill on the area's tourism industry.

That announcement brought immediate condemnation from environmental groups and politicians alike, especially the White House. Why? Because those groups recognize the power of positive messaging via the media and they instantly understood a sustained effort by BP to inform the public as to their on-going commitments and actions to make things right would minimize their adversarial efforts to vilify British Petroleum for their own political and financial gain. (Specifically, raising money and passing environmental legislation.)

In essence, in the same manner BP eventually capped their well, their Media Buys also capped their runaway news crisis by using the *media's own power* to tell their story themselves, rather than allowing their story to be told by others in pursuit of their own agendas.

In producing their PSAs, BP did four more things very well.

First: Accurately identified their vulnerability and their targeted market. Although their secondary market was the nation as a whole (i.e. public opinion), they correctly realized their primary market were the people most directly harmed by their well's oil spill; specifically, the people living and working in the Gulf region.

Second: Having identified their targeted audience, they used local residents within BP's media campaign to relay BP's message to their own neighbors. Who better to reassure the residents that their hometown concerns are being heard and their needs and concerns will be met than other Gulf friends, neighbors, and residents?

Third: Their message was clear. They repeatedly informed the inhabitants of the Gulf Coast that BP was working around the clock to minimize any environmental damages and furthermore, BP would provide cash payments to minimize the financial losses of those businesses affected by their spill, etc.

Fourth: BP went to great lengths to inform Gulf residents (and the public at large) that the oil conglomerate cared about their situation and that they were committed to minimizing any of their personal, commercial and environmental losses. (More on this in Chapter Seven).

Recognizing *how* media works, BP then effectively used those same tools to make that media worked *for* them instead of *against* them! Great Job, BP!

Chapter Six
THE RULES OF ENGAGEMENT

A man far wiser than I once wrote, *Each of us are three people: How we see ourselves, how others see us, and how we really are!*

If you take a moment to think about those words, you can begin to appreciate their simplicity as well as their truthfulness.

It is the *second* of these truisms which we will be addressing.

In Chapter One: Media's Hidden Secrets, I outlined two methods by which the news media can intentionally (or unintentionally) influence the impact of your story, message and media coverage; specifically, "Story Grouping" and "Story Association".

While it is impossible to provide you with a fool-proof method of controlling the decision making of your local news director (that's the individual usually responsible for determining story coverage and placements), you *can* take several steps to minimize the possibilities of negative reporting while maximizing the opportunities to present yourself, your company and your message in the most professional, positive and authoritative manner possible.

And it all begins at the beginning.

Media professionals are people too, and although some of them relish the world of confrontation and conflict, the overwhelming majorities just wish to be treated with respect.

I believe that respect begins at the curb.

Here's our scenario: you have scheduled a press conference at your corporate headquarters.

Some of the worse drudgery of news reporting is the carrying and setting up of the required lights, camera and sound equipment.

Most ENG (Electronic News Gathering) teams consist of only two people: the on-camera talent and his or her camera/audio/lighting technician. Knowing this, you can get the conference off to a great start if you make it possible for those news teams to get in and out of your facilities as quickly and easily as possible.

PRE-CONFERENCE STRATEGIES

Here are some suggestions to accomplish exactly that!

1) Rope off an area for the news vans to park and make sure it is close to an easily accessible entrance to your facility.

2) Assign one or more people to assist them in loading/unloading, arriving and departing the press conference area.

3) Once they have arrived at the press conference, make sure they are greeted with the appropriate amount of refreshments.

Bottled water is always suitable.

However, if your Press Conference is scheduled for the morning hours, coffee, juice and donuts or breakfast pastries are also recommended.

If the afternoon is when your conference is taking place, again bottled water, canned sodas with ice and assorted cookies would be my call.

4) Make sure the area selected for the conference has adequate room (space and height) for the crews to maneuver and set up, and that it is adequately air conditioned.

It is always a good idea to drop the room's temperature by a good five to eight degrees prior to the start of the conference. This is because as soon as the lights and cameras are turned on, the room will heat up rapidly, making it uncomfortable for both them and you!

If you think is some feeble attempt to bribe your press guests into submission, you're wrong!

All you are doing is showing them some professional courtesies, and for the majority of the press corps in attendance, your efforts will not go unnoticed, nor unappreciated.

Think of it this way: if you were to schedule a meeting of marketing professionals to discuss a new public relations or advertisement campaign you're intending to implement in order to bolster your company's public image, wouldn't you have a supply of refreshments for those professionals whom you've invited to sit around your conference table?

Well, each one of those press crews represent the most powerful and effective method of corporate marketing and the molding of public opinion ever conceived by mankind.

Treat them as professionals and most of the time they will return the favor.

CONFERENCE STRATEGIES

In Chapter Four, *My Trilogies of Truth*, I outlined the importance of the following axioms:

    1. Image Equals Perception.

    2. Perception is Reality.

    3. Words are Power.

A Press Conference is the perfect place to put into action all three of these truisms.

Under *Image equals Perception*, I wrote, *The attitude and image you project speaks volumes about the message you're attempting to convey.*

If you project an attitude of self-confidence, it will be perceived as knowledge and authority.

Conversely, if you project an attitude of hesitation or doubt it will be perceived by your audience as weakness, insincerity or even worse, misrepresentation.

I also wrote, *Your appearance is even more important!*

That's because your image is the first word your audience hears and the last word they remember.

And that's where we will begin.

If you are using a corporate spokesperson to represent your company and convey your message, then hopefully you have already followed the guidelines I have outlined in Chapter Four's, trilogy, *Perception is Reality,* and if so, you are already way ahead of the media game.

If however, the press conference is scheduled to be conducted by your company's CEO or president, then I suggest the following techniques be employed to maximize his or hers appearance and impact.

For simplicity of instruction, we will assume you are the one conducting the press conference.

First and foremost, *custom tailor your message!*

A fool-proof method of accomplishing exactly that is fully explained in Chapter Seven, *Knowing Your Audience.*

Many psychologists believe that the average human being forms his or her opinion of someone within *the first fifteen seconds* of meeting them! I believe that to be true and that's why I want your first fifteen seconds to be one of command and authority.

1) Make sure you are dressed appropriately for the audience you are attempting to reach. (Again, reference *Custom Tailoring Your Message,* located in Chapter Seven)

2) Returning to our scenario, when you enter the Press Conference, don't enter alone. Enter with an entourage of your management staff numbering three to five people; again, all dressed appropriately for the audience you are attempting to reach.

3) Do not be the first to enter the room.

Allow two of your staff to lead you to the dais and then have them proceed to a corner of the room where they are close enough to assist you should you ask, but far enough away so as not you diminish your presence as the conference's focal point. Your executive assistant should enter immediately behind you followed by any other staff members you deem appropriate. Your assistant, along with any other staff will join the others in the area away from you and the podium.

4) Your assistant, as well as your staff, should be ready to accept and act upon any direction from you. Should you be asked something you do not know, admit that fact, then turn to the appropriate staff member and instruct (don't ask, instruct) them to get you that information for you by a certain deadline and then instruct the reporter to contact your assistant (acknowledging him or her from the podium) and you will personally see to it the information requested is provided.

These actions project an image of someone who is very much in command and secure enough to acknowledge that although they may not know everything, but they know how to find it out. (It can also buy you some time, if and when needed.)

5) When conducting your interview, I *strongly* urge you to follow *the Kissinger Method* of press conferences as specified in Chapter Five. It will help assure that you will be able to maintain control of the conference itself, maybe not necessarily the questions that will be asked

you, but at least the degree of respect with which they are asked.

6) At the conclusion of the conference thank the members of the Press for coming and the invite them to help themselves to the refreshments.

7) When leaving the conference, unlike your entrance, this time you will lead and your staff will fall in behind you. Each should walk confidently from the room, standing tall and looking sharp.

However, when leaving the press area, it's important to remember, *do not say anything you don't want repeated on the six o'clock news until you are far, far away from the press area.* You never know who is behind you with keen hearing or a recorder.

(I once had a young woman reporter so intent on catching up and speaking with me, without even realizing it, she actually followed me into the men's room and ended up asking me questions while standing next to me at the urinal before realizing where she was. True story!)

CONDUCTING A PRESS CONFERENCE

There is a right and wrong way to conduct a press conference. The following techniques, when used properly, will help you set the tone and maintain control over the participants involved.

A. When conducting your press conferences (or interview) always complement the reporter when he or she asks you an intelligent and poignant question. A simple, *"That's a great question, you've obviously done your homework"* will suffice. Conversely, when asked a ridiculous question, or one obviously meant to intimidate or demean you, do not be afraid to criticize their lack of preparation or professionalism. Something such as, *"You're question is disappointing as you have obviously not taken the time to adequately familiarize yourself with the issues at hand."* The reasoning for this approach is self-explanatory; everyone, especially reporters, love praise and hate criticism. Using this practice sparingly, but appropriately, will help ensure meaningful and constructive interviews.

B. If you want to maximize your air play, it is best to schedule your press conference on a Friday, preferably before noon and provide the reporter with digitized materials in support of your position. That's because most news stations reduce their news staff for the weekend, consequently, if your story plays well and is visually stimulating they are more likely to repeat their best stories over the weekend thereby extending the media coverage of your event. (Reference *MEDIA AIDS* below.

C. However, should you be faced with having to conduct a news conference with the potential of it having a *negative* impact on your company, product, services, or image, then I recommend you schedule it early morning, during the mid-week in hopes that other news stories will quickly render yours old news thus minimizing the potential of your negative exposure.

THE USE OF MEDIA AIDS

Remember, the News Media is in the business of print, images, pictures and sound.

Whatever your topic, if it's important enough to warrant a press conference, it's important enough to warrant some media aids such as photos, audio files and most preferred, video footage. Furthermore, it will serve you better to have those materials available in the form of electronic (digital) files as they allow for minimized image degeneration while being easier to carry and simple to transfer.

Let's assume your conference has been called to announce a new energy efficient method to ensure a plentiful supply of drinking water in times of natural disasters; take time to produce photos to support the need for the process and then visual aids of the process itself for the print press; audio presentations for the radio media and video footage for the television medium.

Taking the time and expense to provide these media aids will help to accomplish the following:

First, professionally produced visual and audio aids will help support your position while greatly increasing the dynamics and impact of your message on your targeted audience.

Second, with impressive visual and audio support materials, your story is far more likely to command *enhanced and prolonged* air and print coverage, as well as a better news position.

Third, and equally important, with you supplying the media materials to visually aid in the telling of your story, your message is likely to be reported more accurately, and that fact alone is worth its weight in gold!

Chapter Seven
KNOWING YOUR AUDIENCE

I'm a little embarrassed to admit I'm mesmerized by those wildlife programs showing how various animals survive in the wild. I'm particularly fascinated by the somewhat uniform social structure all species seem to follow, prey or predator: birth, growth, endurance, death—survival of the fittest.

I'm especially surprised by how often both prey and predator appear to co-exist with each other in relative safety and peace—*provided* the predator part of the equation has recently eaten!

However, I've also noticed there is at least one exception to this rule. It would seem that no matter how full their stomachs may be, if a predator comes across a weakened or injured prey, they'll take them down! It seems to be in their nature to do so.

Now, I have too much respect for my fellow professionals to draw a *direct* comparison between reporter and the reported with predators and their prey. But it is one of life's lessons that warrant remembering.

Simply stated, never show fear or weakness, because a good reporter (or audience) will sense it and go for your throat!

STRUCTURING YOUR MESSAGE

So many well intentioned and competent executives are so consumed with the big picture, they fail to recognize that often times, the most effective stories are told frame-by-frame.

It is also extremely important to remember, while the media allows you to tell your story to vast numbers of people, and to do so all at the same time, your words are always addressing that audience on a one-to-one basis, and that's a good thing!

Allow me to explain. If you are delivering a message to 10,000 people in an auditorium, how effectively your message is received by the individuals comprising that audience will be substantially influenced by how the crowd as a whole reacts to your speech.

This is precisely why Hollywood inserts laugh tracks in their Sitcoms in order to "inform" their audiences as to what's funny and just how funny it is supposed to be. The laugh tracks are extremely effective and help drive the comedic impact of their programs.

Real-life Media works the same way.

In Chapter One, I discussed how in the earliest days of radio and then television, America was mesmerized by the phenomenon of listening (and eventually watching) Hollywood celebrities and their world leaders in the comfort of their own living rooms! For the first time, this new form of Electronic Media gave audiences a sense of personal connection to the stories, events, and personalities of the day.

The audiences reached by those programs may have topped tens of millions, but every successful entertainer, broadcaster, and politician recognized he or she was only speaking to an audience of one!

You must strive to do the same.

I have developed three seemingly simple, yet really quite complex questions designed to accomplish exactly that! Answer these questions correctly and you will be successful in reaching and delivering your message correctly, effectively, efficiently and succinctly, each time and every time.

> Question One: *Who am I trying to reach?*
> Question Two: *What do I want them to know?*
> Question Three: *What do I want them to do or feel?*

Sound simple? Well, if it does, then you're not giving these questions enough thought.

Ninety-eight percent of the time, when I sit down with clients to discuss the intricacies of these questions, they end up changing the focus of their message *for the better!*

Let's examine them one at a time.

Question One:
WHO DO YOU WANT TO REACH?

If you've taken the time to read my biography, you found that I spend a large portion of my adult life working as a producer, writer, and director for television networks such as A&E, The Biography Channel, The History Channel and others.

However, for me, the very best of both worlds is when I am given the opportunity to marry my artistry with some down to earth pragmatism in order to help private sector clients use media effectively for all the right reasons.

In that role, I have been privileged, and that is the correct word—*privileged*—to assist both individuals and organizations who have dedicated their lives to the service of others. Many of whose faces they may never see, and whose voices they may never hear, but none the less, they have dedicated every one of their waking hours to helping those in need, both here at home and around the world.

One such client, based on the East Coast, provides the unique service of soliciting discarded or obsolete (by Western standards) medical equipment and supplies from local hospitals. They eagerly accept everything from individual examining tables and diagnostic equipment, to fully equipped operating rooms and treatment centers. Once they receive these life-saving materials, they test, repair and refurbish the equipment and then provided it free to needy doctors, medical clinics and hospitals throughout the world.

You have to witness it firsthand to fully appreciate what they do to help the world's needy, and they do all for free!

When I first met with them, they wanted help in developing a media message for the purpose of, you guessed it, raising money.

They truly work their miracles on a shoestring budget through a combination of word-of-mouth equipment donations and hundreds of volunteers coordinated through local community and charitable organizations. But no matter how many people they are helping, there is always so much more to accomplish.

Consequently, when I asked them "Who do you want to reach?" they replied, "People with money to donate to our cause and help fund our on-going operations."

However, after meeting with them for several hours and discussing both their immediate and long term goals and objectives, it became obvious to me, they didn't need to reach *one* group of people, they actually needed to reach *three* separate groups of people.

First, they needed to reach hospital administrators throughout the region and educate them to the fact that hospitals no longer had to pay excessive hazardous waste materials charges to local land fills in order to rid themselves of their obsolete medical equipment as there was now an organization willing to accept their discards for free; and then put that equipment back into service treating those in need.

Second, since what they do is very labor intensive (i.e. accepting equipment and materials, disassembling it, inspecting it, cleaning it, repairing it, re-assembling it, labeling and then packaging it and making it ready for shipment), in order to keep their overhead low, all those labor intensive activities are performed by volunteers. Consequently, they also needed to get their message out to those companies, groups and organizations which encourage and support the volunteer efforts of their employees.

Third, and finally, without question, they did have a real need to solicit new and renewable sources of outside funding to help support their basic operational expenses.

The end result was to develop one message focusing on what they do and how they do it with *three* separate "heads" (openings) and *three* separate "tails" (endings).

One of the beginnings and subsequent tails targeted hospital administrators; the second targeted administrators of the various local volunteer organizations, together with the CEOs of companies known for their community commitments; and the third one was directed specifically to charitable funding individuals and entities.

Consequently, while each presentation has a different opening and closing (depending upon whether the message was asking for discarded medical equipment or supplies, volunteer support, or charitable funding), the body of the message (the one that demonstrated what they did and how they did it) remained the same in all three presentations.

Usually, you only have one shot at making your case, so think it through thoroughly and use that opportunity wisely.

That's why it is so important to define your ultimate goals and objectives as well as the specific demographics of your targeted audience!

IDENTIFYING YOUR AUDIENCE

This is so key to the success of your message, that when I ask clients, *who do you want to reach?* I suggest they think about it overnight before answering it.

But for those who answer too quickly, these are a few of their more common responses: *the general public!* or *our stockholders* or *our customers, potential customers, potential donors,* etc. You get the picture.

Before I get into the true substance of this chapter, I feel it is important to state the obvious.

Once you have accurately determined your targeted audience, you need to tailor both *the messenger* and *the message* to that specific target.

For instance, if your target audiences are teenagers, you wouldn't choose a fifty year old spokesperson; conversely, if you are trying to penetrate the over fifty crowd, you wouldn't have a teenage spokesperson.

Consequently, when selecting an individual to represent you, your products or services to your potential customers, remember, two previously stated key factors;

First, *Perception is Reality.*

Second, *Psychologists believe that the average human being forms his or her opinion of someone within the first fifteen seconds of meeting them.* So make sure your spokesperson dresses, speaks and acts in a way that is appealing to the audiences you are attempting to reach.

(However, when it comes to suggested techniques to be used in the construction of your actual message, I will refer you to the next section entitled, *What Do You Want Them to Know?*

For now, let's continue with the importance of accurately determining, *Who Do You Want to Reach?*

This type of analysis always seems to work best when we set it up a scenario from which all of us can work. So here it is:

The following is a factual depiction of actual events.

Because I don't think it's appropriate to disclose client's names, suffice it to say, an extremely well-known, Fortune 500 company came to me for the purpose of developing a more effective method of marketing a high-ticketed item they were selling to a very specific targeted audience.

Although the product was by no means a new one, their concept of how to market it was ingenious.

Here is where it gets interesting.

As mentioned, they are a very large company with the resources to research their potential customers thoroughly.

The average cost of the products they were selling ranged from $25,000 on the low end to $40,000 plus on the high end.

Their experience and research had shown their primary targeted audiences were women in their late forties to early fifties and men from their mid to late fifties.

Easy enough. Correct? Here's the twist!

Their research went on to show—ready for this?—*their research went on to show women in their late forties and early fifties had an image of themselves as being in their mid thirties to late thirties!*

Men in their mid to late fifties had an image themselves as being in their early-forties!

Consequently, when it came time to hire the actors needed to represent their products to their targeted audiences (specifically, women in their late forties to early fifties and men from their mid to late fifties), *I hired an actress in her mid thirties and an actor in his early-forties!*

The result was nothing less than spectacular as the end results far exceed the client's expectations!

The lesson to be learned here is *it is not good enough to know the demographics of your targeted audience, it also important to know how your targeted audiences perceive themselves!*

Question Two:
WHAT DO YOU WANT THEM TO KNOW?

It's been proven time and time again, the most successful method of delivering an effective message is through simple, clear, concise, and strong statements.

Examples would includes such declarations as, *Mass Media Molds The Minds of Modern Man, Miracles exist, Failure is not an option, Today is the first day of the rest of your life!* I'm sure you get the idea.

However, it is also important to tailor your message in an understandable manner. Being too fact-filled or too complex will only confuse your audience and either bore them or anger them, either of which spells trouble for you.

When making your case, whether it be to the working press or to your staff, focus on the minimum number of issues (generally, I suggest a maximum of three) needed to make your argument persuasive.

Furthermore, always be cognizant of the reality, *people react best to those issues that affect them most!"*

In other words, *personalize* your issues so your audiences will react to them on an *individual* basis.

The six greatest motivators in this area are any issues that will:

    1. Threaten their health or safety.

    2. Improve their quality of life.

    3. Re-affirm their hopes and dreams.

    4. Excuse their failures.

    5. Make, cost, or save them money.

    6. Obstruct their needs, desires, or comfort.

Keep reading and you will witness first hand, the correct and *incorrect* way to package your message.

Question Three:
WHAT DO YOU WANT THEM TO FEEL?

One of my clients is a Municipality which is facing a potentially severe shortage of life's most precious commodity—water!

Fortunately, the individuals charged with planning for the city's future needs have recognized that fact and have designed and implemented a remarkable, cutting-edge program designed to solve the crisis *before* it can negatively impact its citizenry's standard of living., not to mention the city's economy.

That's the good news, the bad news is that the new program will result in higher water costs.

In a planning meeting it was suggested that the public be made aware of the pending rate increases through a press release to be made available to all appropriate news outlets.

The city's press relations person's suggested release was entitled *Water Cost Increase Expected in Fall.* The article went on to emphasize that even though necessity dictated that water rates in the city would increase in the coming fall, even with the proposed rate hikes, the new price for water would remain amongst the lowest in the county.

Pretty straight forward, but guaranteed to ignite a fire storm (no pun intended) amongst the city council's business and agricultural constituents.

My suggestion was to take a slightly different approach.

I advised the City to release a press story that first acknowledged the threat of a coming water shortage; followed by an explanation of the program the city's planners had devised to avoid that shortage and in turn, ensure a continual, safe and dependable water supply for the city and its residents; and third then mention a slight increase in water rates would be necessary, but the alternative was simply not acceptable.

My suggested headline?

City Running Out of Water.

All I did was take the *same* information as contained in the proposed press release announcing the rate hike, and re-formulate it into a message that initially *threatened the reader's safety* and potentially *impeded their future comfort*.

Who Do You Want To Reach?

Those needed to be reached were reached.

In this case the primary audience was the local business and agricultural communities as well as the city's residents;

What Do You Want Them To Know?

In this case, our message was that the city needed to increase their water rates in order to prevent a pending water shortfall; and

What Do You Want Them To Do?

We wanted them to willingly accept a utilities price increase in order to fund a major revamping of the city's water collections and distribution system.

The result was more than any of us could have hoped. Both the print and electronic media gave it prime play, front page above the fold, and lead stories on both local radio and television outlets.

Not only did the constituents accept the cost increases, but they did so while praising the city's planners for their foresight and planning.

Mission accomplished!

Chapter Eight
THE TEN COMMANDMENTS OF COMMUNICATION

Before we begin, and even though I know you've heard this before (because I've said it before), it is still worth both repeating and remembering, *Image isn't everything, it's the only thing!*

Consequently, whenever and to whomever you deliver your message *always* be fully cognizant of your appearance as well as your surroundings because it is the first and last thing your audiences will remember.

Now, on to the topic at hand.

At an early age, I was surprised to read that one of the greatest fears shared by most corporate leaders is having to get up in front of an audience and speak. I found that unexpected, because, although I am the proud owner of a plethora of fears, public speaking isn't one of them.

Consequently, if you are one of those individuals who fears speaking in public (much less facing hostile reporters at a press conference), I'm confident the following techniques will transform your inner anxieties into enjoyable experiences.

So let's get to it!

The First Commandment of Communication
AUDIENCE INVOLVEMENT

How many times have you attended a conference where a string of speakers have gone on and on and on until your posterior starts falling asleep? Yet, if one of those speakers involves you or any member of the audience in his or her presentation, a wave of energy is instantly injected into the room—and the audience!

You may be saying, "Well that's great providing your audience is small enough to reach on that level."

The truth is, the size of your audience plays no part in this equation and I'll explain why.

Obliviously, if you are addressing a smaller group of people, it is much easier to involve them in your presentation by engaging them in conversation by asking them questions and evoking responses to your ideas and directives.

But in many ways, interaction with large audiences can be easier than interfacing with smaller and more intimate groups, and here's how.

A while back I was asked to participate in a public relations seminar for a rather large and somewhat elite group of professionals from both the business and political sectors. It was made clear to me my time would be limited to two hours. Needless to say, I wanted to make a great impression, but more importantly, I wanted my presentation to have an impact on as many of those attendees as possible.

Since I knew my audience would consist of some of corporate America's best known movers and shakers, I was also aware people of such stature are usually reluctant to openly participate in group discussions. Consequently, I employed the following tactic.

As part of their registration packet, I requested the sponsoring organization to include a simple questionnaire asking participants the following: *Please list in their order of importance, the three most important techniques you would like to learn in order to more deal more effectively with the news media.*

Since my presentation was scheduled for late afternoon, that morning I collected the completed forms and spent the next several hours going through them and learning which topics were of the greatest interest to my audience.

Consequently, when it came time for my presentation, I was able to tailor make it to address the specific needs of my audience. The result was that I was able to immediately capture and hold their undivided attention throughout my entire two-hour session because I was targeting their specific requests and questions, thus providing them with meaningful answers with which the majority of the audience could identify and utilize.

With each of the speakers who preceded me, although the information they disseminated may have been pertinent and extremely useful, it was too generalized to activity engage and maintain the audience's attention and interaction on an individual basis. Consequently, that fact alone made it difficult for their audiences to remain engaged.

Conversely, my presentation addressed those precise topics and questions which I knew to be pertinent to a large contingent of my audience.

Furthermore, prior to answering them, I made it a point to announce the various questions and desired objectives of their fellow professionals to the general audience, knowing that many of them would take those inquiries and concerns to heart as information they may need to know as well.

The results were predictable. Because, for that two hour period, the specific questions and needs of a large portion of that audience were anonymously addressed and answered, the information provided proved meaningful for all in attendance and that made for a great experience for both student and teacher.

The Second Commandment of Communication
HUMOR

Ask yourself, *What is God's greatest gift to mankind?*

When I have asked that of my audiences, the first answer is usually *Love*. Love is great, but unfortunately, often times it is accompanied by the pain of heartbreak.

Personally, I've always believed God's greatest gift to mankind is laughter!

To me, laughter is the universal language. How can anyone feel bad when they're laughing?

But, please keep in mind, humor is a very sharp sword capable cutting both ways, so you need to use it carefully.

Add to that reality, the safest form of humor is always the self-deprecating kind.

Consequently, whether you are short or tall, fat, bald or skinny, young or old, strikingly handsome or aesthetically challenged, it is always safe to make fun of yourself.

Another case in point: For ten years in a row, I was privileged to serve as the Director for a live awards show known as *The Golden Boot Awards* which had occurred annually for twenty-five years in support of the Motion Picture and Television Fund; one of my industry's more respected charities.

The awards program honors entertainment legends who have contributed to Hollywood's Western filmmaking.

In 2003, our Golden Boot honoree was Oscar winner, Tommy Lee Jones.

Picture this: the International Ballroom of The Beverly Hilton Hotel in Beverly Hills, is filled with between eight hundred and a thousand people (all of whom have paid an average of $400 per ticket) to see and honor Tommy Lee along with a variety of other film and entertainment celebrities.

As mentioned, the program is live! Meaning, once I cue the opening music, the show starts and runs straight through to the end, no matter what happens!

About half way through the night's festivities, I hear over my headset that our star celebrity, Tommy Lee Jones has collapsed at his table and has been taken to The Green

Room (a room off the stage where talent gathers prior to going on stage).

I immediately make my way to the green room.

When I enter, the first thing I see is Tommy sitting on a couch with his head down; his hands in his lap and a nurse taking his blood pressure. The nurse quietly reports to me that his blood pressure is fine but he is running a slight fever and feeling light-headed.

Tommy Lee Jones is the consummate professional. He recognizes that he is there to support The Motion Picture and Television Fund and that there is a ballroom full of people who have paid a lot of money to honor him.

Consequently, he is feeling very embarrassed about the whole situation and I sense that the last place he wants to be is in that Green Room, feeling poorly and surrounded by strangers.

To make him feel more at ease, I needed to break that tension, so standing in front of him and with him staring at the floor (i.e. my feet), I said in a commanding voice, "Well, Tommy, I think we can safely rule out possibility that you are simply overcome with excitement at the opportunity of meeting me!"

You could hear a pin drop.

His wife grinned and he slowly raised his head, smiled and said, "Oh, I don't know, I'm feeling pretty excited."

With his smile, the tension in the room was immediately broken and everyone, including Tommy Lee felt more at ease.

The nurse surmised that Tommy was coming down with a bad case of the Flu, but being the professional he is, he wanted to go on away. I changed the show's line-up and got him on stage as quickly as possible and then had his car brought around to the back so he and his wife could leave through a private exit.

That momentary attempt at self-deprecating humor let him know, as the show's Director, I wasn't stressing out and whatever we needed to do, it would be fine.

Humor is a valuable ice-breaker and stress reliever; however, I recommend when using it, do so without using profanities. More often than not, off-color language offends more people than it entertains. You shouldn't need to use vulgarities to make someone laugh, and if you do, you need new material!

Nevertheless, when used appropriately, humor can be an extremely effective method of humanizing yourself to your audience and helping them relate to, sympathize with and/or accept you for whom you are.

The Third Commandment of Communication
FEAR

While in college, I took numerous public speaking courses and quickly learned that the easiest way to command the attention of my fellow students was to select topics, the substance of which, could have either a direct *positive* or *negative* impact on their individual lives; topics such as techniques on how to improve their academic

standings; or which of life's careers choices were more lu-
crative or how to improve their finances. Or conversely, I
would focus on some of life's more negative consequences
such as the most dangerous mistakes travelers can make,
and/or what not to do when buying a car.

The reason invoking fear is such a powerful communication tool is because it carries with it a negative or
threatening connotation; and anything threatening to us is
guaranteed to capture and hold our attention.

Obliviously, the fear factor can't, nor should it be used
in every presentation, but when appropriate, you'll find it
very effective in commanding your audience's attention and
thus making it easier for you to communicate your message.

Although fear is one of the most powerful factors, it is
not the only factor you can utilized to capture and hold an
audience's attention. As stated previously in Chapter Seven,
Know Your Audience, if you can wrap your presentation
around any of the following themes, you will easily capture
the eyes and ears of your spectators.

Topics designed to improve their quality of life, re-
affirm their hopes and dreams and—here is a really big
crowd pleaser—topics that allow audiences to excuse their
personal failures in life.

Whether appearing before a live audience or a bank of
news cameras, if you follow that same formula you will
have a much higher success rate of reaching your targeted

audience, holding their attention and convincing them of your position.

The Fourth Commandment of Communication
PASSION

The word *passion* is defined as "a powerful emotion or deep burning desire." But for the public speaker or corporate spokesperson, the term *passion* should also be defined as "a belief in or a commitment to."

It's a simple secret, *Believe in your message, and your audience will believe in you!*

Why? Because when you truly believe in what you are saying (or selling) there is something in the human spirit that automatically kicks in and when it does, every part of your body and soul joins in your presentation. Your body movements project confidence, your voice delivers your message in a more believable manner, your eyes begin to twinkle, and if a smile on your face is appropriate, it will come naturally.

In my business, it's quite common for me to direct voice overs (VOs—the recording of separate narration tracks) for use in the various television programs and commercials I produce.

More often than not, this requires a man or woman to sit alone in a sound-proof recording booth and read the narrative script needed to facilitate the program's theme and images.

I mention this because, in that somewhat creatively sterile environment, it continually amazes me how the tone quality of the narrator's voice changes for the better when they read their lines while smiling (assuming of course the subject matter supports that form of emotion).

If your subject is of a more somber or threatening nature, then allow your face to express that seriousness and your voice will follow suite.

That's why it is so important to *believe* in what you're saying.

But what if you don't in the message you are trying to sell?

If you ever find yourself in a position where you cannot intellectually, morally, or spiritually support the position you are being asked to represent, then do yourself and your company a favor and help find someone who does and then train *them* to articulate the position.

To do anything else would only foster insincerely; and insincerity weakens your credibility. And as a Media spokesperson, your credibility is your single greatest asset.

The Fifth Commandment of Communication
ENERGY

We've all attended presentations asking ourselves, *How much longer do we have to sit through this?* Yet, those thoughts rarely occur when that presentation is delivered in an enthusiastic and energetic manner.

But how does one emote energy to audiences in an effective manner? The answer? It begins as soon as you step up to the plate. With what? Your Image!

Are you dressed in a way that relates to your audience and projects confidence and authority? That doesn't necessarily mean a three button, Brooks Brothers suit, but it does mean the clothes you are wearing need to be clean, pressed, starched, color coordinated and professionally appropriate.

On many occasions when I have given a seminar or lecture using a chalkboard or similar equipment, I've begun by asking the audience's permission to remove my coat to allow me a greater freedom of movement while writing on the board.

That gesture immediately creates a working, participatory environment rather than a passive, listening one; and audiences react appropriately.

When the surroundings and conditions allow, during your presentation don't remain in one place but rather move around in order to better interact with your audience.

So many people allow the microphone to dictate where they must stand. But today, most microphones are wireless allowing them to be worn, removed, or carried.

Speaking for myself, more often than not, I prefer to substitute the comfort of the microphone for the ability to move freely around the stage or throughout the room. (This assumes, of course, that if no wireless microphone is available, your voice is strong enough to clearly reach every individual to whom you are addressing).

Two additional powerful forms of energy are eye contact and silence. Allow me to explain.

It is universally agreed, when addressing the press or an audience, always keep your eyes up, facing your addressees and then, if necessity dictates for you to look down at your notes, do so for no more than a momentary glance.

A speaker (or interviewee) who seldom looks up at their audience (or interviewer) cannot and will not command their respect or their attention. It is as simple as that.

However, there is also a general misconception that when speaking to a large audience, you should allow your eyes to scan that audience. In my opinion, scanning an audience means you are purposely avoiding eye contact and nature tells us when someone purposely avoids looking you squarely in the eye, they usually have something to hide.

I mentioned earlier that if you have passion in your presentation, your eyes will show it, so let your eyes help tell your story.

Here are some tips to help accomplish exactly that.

1) During your presentation, make personal eye contact with *numerous* people throughout *every* section of the room.

2) The actual contact should be limited to only a few moments at a time. Follow your instincts, when it begins to feel uncomfortable for them, or for you,

move on to the next person and in doing so, *your eyes will walk the room.*

3) Another good technique to remember is when you are ready to make a key point, don't hold on one person; as you finish your thoughts share those points and implant your ideas in the eyes of two or three additional people.

Silence may be golden but it is also extremely potent and inspiring when used appropriately.

I remember reading an interview with the then rising star Michael J. Fox, an actor whose on screen presence I have always found to be both natural and memorable. In that interview he said something which I have never forgotten and have past on to many of the actors with whom I've worked.

When asked to what he attributed his meteoric-rise on the hit television series that made him a rising star, *Family Ties,* he answered, and I am paraphrasing, *because I realized that when the camera is on an actor, that actor is in complete and total control on that scene. And if I used those opportunities to insert some pauses in my lines, the scenes themselves carried more of an impact and that gave my character a greater screen presence.*

I agree with every syllable of that.

Too many people, whether they are standing in front of a news camera or an audience, are intent on racing through their answers or presentations. This is a natural instinct that rises from fear: fear of making a mistake or a fear of boring their audiences.

On the contrary, the use of an appropriate amount and length of pregnant pauses within your presentation will only draw attention to both you and what you are saying, because attention always equates to energy!

People come pre-programmed to listen for a methodic rhythm of speech. When you interrupt that anticipated rhythm with a few well placed pauses, the effect is to peak your audiences curiosity, thus enhancing their levels of alertness and thus, their levels of energy!

The Sixth Commandment of Communication
KNOW YOUR SUBJECT MATTER

I can't count the number of times I've had friends come to me and say they've been asked to give a work-related 30 minute presentation and the first question out of their mouth is, *How in the world am I going to fill thirty minutes of time?* I know how they feel because once I asked that same question of myself.

I remember my first paid speech. I was in my early twenties and when I received the booking slip, it stated that they were requesting that my presentation last for 45 minutes, followed by a question and answer session.

FORTY-FIVE MINUTES!!!!!

My first thought was, *How am I going to fill forty-five minutes of time, much less make it interesting as well?*

In preparing for that task, I ended up learning a very valuable and comforting lesson. Specifically, the more knowledgeable you are about every aspect of the subject on which you will be speaking, the easier and more interesting your presentation will be, *no matter what the length!*

Once I had learned everything I could regarding my subject matter, my question quickly changed to, *How do I fit all I want to say in only 45 minutes?*

My syndicated radio news feature *Face to Face* was a program produced in advance of its airing dates and then delivered to stations throughout the country and around the world for broadcast. On several occasions, I was invited by many of these stations to guest host their live, on-the-air talk programs.

I grew to love doing this.

To me, the challenges of live radio, instant debates and audience interactions, always proved invigorating, to say the least.

But once again I faced that initial question . . . *How do I hope to fill three hours of live radio, day after day, while still leaving my audiences wanting more?*

Clearly, the key to the success of those live programs was twofold: first researching a selection of topics that would be of interest to my audiences; and second, learning as much information as possible on each of the topics I wanted to cover, information either in my head or at my finger tips. That's because, information is not only powerful, but when presented in the correct manner, using many of the points already discussed (i.e., humor, passion, energy, fear, etc.). Knowledge is also energizing and entertaining!

I realize what I am about to say seems simplistic, but that doesn't make it any less truthful.

If you are ever asked to prepare for an interview, or a presentation of *any* length, and you begin by worrying about how you're going to fill the time, you're not properly prepared! If on the other hand, when you begin preparing your speech, lecture, seminar, or presentation and you start wondering about how are you ever going to cover *all* your points within the given time restraints, you're ready for anything that comes your way!

Case in point; One the very first people to ever appear on my radio program, *Face to Face* was then legendary comedian and stage, radio, television and film star, Bob Hope.

The interview was conducted in his office located in the "business" wing of his home (more like a compound) in Toluca Lake, California (a very fashionable part of the San Fernando Valley).

After setting up our recording equipment, we were informed by one of his staff that "Mr. Hope will arrive shortly." It was then that I notice the then entertainment icon was already there, just outside the door, nervously pacing back and forth, seemingly reluctant to come in and join us.

This went on for a good ten minutes when finally, he quickly turned, entered the room, grabbed a golf club and sat down in his favorite chair across from me.

I should remind you here that *Face to Face* was a *radio* program, and radio requires verbalization.

A typical radio interview for *Face to Face* consisted of between twenty to thirty questions and required about thirty minutes to complete with each of the interviewee's answers lasting an average of forty-five to sixty seconds in length. I would soon learn Bob Hope was *not* going to be a typical interview.

After twenty minutes and *eighty-seven* questions later, I still didn't have one single answer I could actually use on the program. It didn't seem to matter how I phrased my questions, he always answered in short, two or three word sentences; not enough for me to actually build a radio program around.

That continued until when out of desperation, I asked him why early in his show business career he chose to become an amateur boxer and fight under the name Packy East.

It was as if a switch had been turned on inside him and the Bob Hope the entertainment legend the world had come to know and love, awakened before my very eyes. From that point forward, his answers were filled with information, enthusiasm and humor and I ended up with one terrific program.

I later realized, like many entertainers, Bob Hope *the person* was a very shy man. And even though in the coming years, Bob would end up appearing numerous times on my program, that afternoon was the first time we had met. I knew *him* as Bob Hope; he did know *me* from Adam. (By the way, the answer to my question why he boxed under the name Pack East was in order to help him pay his rent. The yet undiscovered comic genius would routinely put on boxing gloves and go a few rounds with a string of amateur boxers. He chose the ring name Packy East because his roommate was doing the same thing and fighting under the name Packy West.)

He went on to share with me and my audience a string of hilarious behind the scene stories of his success and failures as an entertainer, golfer and businessman.

My salvation was taking the time to thoroughly research my subject matter.

I knew about Bob Hope's boxing career because I had researched "Bob the Man" as well as "Bob the Entertainer." Consequently, after running through every question I could think of on topics I wanted to talk about, with my "Packy East" question, I had stumbled on to something *he* wanted to talk about. That broke the ice and the interview was pure gold from that point forward.

What's the morale of the story? There is no substitute for knowledge!

Knowing your subject matter will give you confidence, and in turn, that confidence will allow you to step up to the podium, or on to a stage, and tailor your presentation to *any* length, in *any* situation and to *any* audience.

The Seventh Commandment of Communication
EXAMPLES

In Chapter Four, *My Trilogies of Truth,* I gave a specific example of how third party testimonials have a far greater impact on the psyche of your audiences than a simple series of self-adulations.

There is a reason for that.

Examples give your audiences *permission* to agree with your point of view.

Think about that for a moment.

It is very rare in the human psyche to find individuals willing to go against the crowd.

If you are a corporate leader, or one who wants to be, then there is a high probability that you're already one of those people who thinks out of the box and who is not afraid to step forward to promote your ideas and display your leadership.

But how many of your colleagues exhibit those exact *opposite* traits? Whether they realize it or not, the vast majority of humanity seek permission for *what they think and how they act;* and more often than not, they derive that permission from the observed actions of those around them; especially those whom they respect or admire or those designated as specialists or experts (many times, self-designated).

Remember how laugh tracks are effectively used in the production of television Sitcoms? (Chapter Seven). Their positioning, length, and intensity informs the audience (thus providing permission through example) as to when, how long, and how hard to laugh at the writer's jokes!

I am not saying people can't think for themselves.

They can and do draw their own conclusions on a wide variety of issues but usually only on those issues which they deem important or have a direct impact on *themselves*. In life's general scheme, a majority of the world's population finds it a great deal easier to simply go along with the crowd.

That's why it's so important to use examples in the presentation of a persuasive argument.

The totality of your facts, opinions and points of view may be very impressive, but what the majority of audiences are searching for are reasons to either *agree* or *disagree* with your points of view. Consequently, one or more well-chosen examples of empirical evidence supporting your ideas and concepts will go a long way in providing your audiences the permission so many want, seek and need.

The use of some well-chosen "Examples" within your presentation will make your argument easier to understand and even easier to support.

The Eighth Commandment of Communication
IMAGERY

The magic of audio and visual imagery is not limited to the impact of sights and sounds alone. Imagery, or more precisely, the ability to *create* imagery, is governed only by the limitations of the body's five senses: sight, sound, touch, taste, and smell.

Let's begin with the art of verbalizing imagery.

As already demonstrated, words are powerful and when used appropriately can evoke fear, instill calm, arouse suspicion, or instill pride or confidence.

Recently, I had the opportunity to listen to a conversation on the radio between national talk show host Dennis Prager and his guest, the Chief Rabbi of the British Commonwealth, Lord Jonathan Sachs. The topic was how a country's citizenry can best identify with their heritage. During that discussion, the rabbi made a very interesting observation. He pointed out that throughout England there exists a plethora of statues commemorating British historic figures and each of those statues displays is the person's name and the years in which they lived.

He then compared Britain's statues to the monuments that grace our nation's capitol, Washington, DC. Naturally, our statues are primarily of America's historic figures (Lincoln, Jefferson, etc.) but our nation's tributes to our historic figures also include depictions of the *words and writings* of these great Americans: *We hold these truths to be self-evident (Jefferson); A government of the people, by the people, for the people shall not perish (Lincoln); With malice toward none, with charity for all (Lincoln);* etc.

The rabbi's point was in order to instill pride in a nation's history, those individuals who helped write that history should be remembered and honored together with their thoughts, deeds and commitments rather than simply the years that mark their existence.

Again, the rabbi's remarks re-emphasize the truism that words are powerful, and here are several ways you can put power to work for you.

MENTAL IMAGERY

In its heyday, radio was known as *the theater of the mind,* and truer words are rarely spoken.

Why? Because when used properly, words create mental images within the boundaries of your mind, *whether you want them too or not!*

Allow me to demonstrate.

You're driving along in your car listening to the radio when you hear a news flash, *The Eiffel Tower has collapsed under its own weight and is now lying on its side"*

Instantaneously, your mind automatically visualizes that image in your brain. You didn't have to consciously construct it—it just happened.

That's because, when used diligently, words can and do involuntarily trigger immediate reactions, images, and emotions deep within the recesses of your mind.

Consequently, when stating your position or addressing an issue, whether it's before a friendly audience; a hostile audience or even the dreaded news media, always take the time to use those words that evoke clear, active and sympathetic imagery in support of your advocacy.

SPEECH IMAGERY

Another effective example of how to utilize clear imagery in the forging of convincing arguments is figures of speech.

When used properly, they have the ability to drive home your points in a non-threatening manner. That's because *we're coming to a fork in the road* is more disarming, thus more persuasive, than *it's time for you to make a decision!* Or *we travel life's journey on our own paths* is far more palatable than *I don't care whether you agree with me or not!* Or saying something such as, *a light went off in my head* can make you sound more human, less stubborn and open to new ideas and concepts.

VISUAL IMAGERY

There was a time that the term *visual imagery* would have almost certainly translated into slides and charts, but in today's world, the term can mean everything from video conferencing to inter-active websites; from animated clips to music driven video presentations and Webinars. My point is, while in some cases, charts and slides may still be appropriate, today's audiences demand to be *entertained* while being *educated* so always be open to using every tool at your disposal to accomplish exactly that!

As previously mentioned, words aren't the only tools that create imagery. All of the human five senses possess the power to persuade, so when possible utilize them all!

The Sense of Sound

In my industry, Sound is equated a value. For instance, generally speaking, if a client pays to run a commercial on television and that commercial runs without sound, they are entitled to a rebate of forty percent.

Ever watch a slap-stick comedy with the sound off? The impacts of the comedic effects are dramatically reduced once the accompanying sound effects are removed. The same goes for your presentation.

The proper music can make or break your performance in the very same way a film score can dramatically contribute to the success of a feature film.

However, a more subtle use of sound can also be extremely effective.

Recently I was privileged to be given a private tour of the *USS Missouri* in Pearl Harbor, Hawaii. The official who gave me the tour mentioned their on-going efforts to make various historic areas of the ship as real as possible to the visiting Public. One area in particular they were working on is the ship's Combat Information Center or the CIC. Their task? What would be a cost-effective method to make the Public more easily identify with the day-to-day workings of this mighty Battleship? My suggestion? A sound track depicting the true-to-life activities of the center during an all-out attack. Allowing people to hear the actions taking place will trigger their minds to automatically create the appropriate action-oriented visual realities.

A complete audio-visual approach to the problem would be preferred, however, audio props alone can be extremely effective, and far less costly.

The Sense of Taste

This method seems pretty self-evident. One cannot enter a Supermarket without presenters or demonstrators offering you the latest in cheeses, fruit drinks, and micro-waved goodies. If your product or presentations lend themselves to the taste test, do it, just be sure your audience will find your product or refreshment as delightful as you do.

If the size of your audience makes that impossible, then try this next technique.

The Sense of Smell

Olfaction is one of the mind's most powerful triggers.

If you've ever attended a Trade Show, then you most likely have already experienced its power, first hand.

Two of the most frequently used aroma factors are popcorn and Starbucks coffee followed closely by any bakery products.

When walking through a trade show or convention center, those booths or participants offering popcorn (by popping it on the spot) or Starbuck's coffee (by brewing it on the spot) are not doing so to be gracious; they are doing so because the aroma permeates the immediate areas thus attracting crowds. And within those crowds are potential new customers!

The Sense of Touch

Again, the sense of Touch is one of the body's most powerful persuaders.

This is one of those times where a simple example speaks volumes. While traveling through Salt Lake City with my then young adult children, we happened upon the *Titanic* road exhibit.

The three of us went through the display and were deeply moved by the artifacts and human stories. As impressed as I was however, what captured my attention more than anything else was the very last exhibit before the exit. They had a wall of ice with an area to place your hand. They wanted you to feel just how cold the water was in which so many lost their life.

For that short moment, you felt what they felt.

It was bone-chilling and obviously something I will never forget.

Keep in mind, whether you're addressing a select group of spectators or the public-at-large (via the Media) today's audiences have been spoiled by the impressive and ever expanding explosion of 21st century communications. Consequently, when and where possible, you need to use those same tools in support of your argument and positions, because today's audiences have come to expect nothing less! (And besides, if you don't, there's a very good chance your competition will!)

Let your imagination be your guide!

The Ninth Commandment of Communication
RECOGNIZABLE QUOTATIONS

In Chapter One, under the subtext, *Media's Second Principle of Power*, I outlined how media's use of story association can have either a positive or negative impact on how stories are reported.

In a similar way, the use of recognizable quotations within *your* presentation can serve as your own private form of story association.

Chosen properly, and used sparingly, appropriate quotations from accomplished individuals will add both credibility to your thoughts and confidence to your delivery.

It doesn't matter what the subject matter of your presentation or conference may be, whether it's economics, science or business, nationalism or internationalism, or simply confronting life's challenges, the selected use of a respected authoritarian source to support your position automatically associates you or your thoughts, with that individual and the respect they command.

Here are some of my favorites:

On Liberty

You can protect your liberties in this world only by protecting the other man's freedom. You can be free only if I am free.

Clarence Darrow

Educate and inform the whole mass of the people. They are the only sure reliance for the preservation of our liberty.

Thomas Jefferson

The Constitution is not an instrument for the government to restrain the people; it is an instrument for the people to restrain the government—lest it come to dominate our lives and interests.

Patrick Henry

On Success

He that is good for making excuses is seldom good for anything else.

Benjamin Franklin

To succeed in life, you need two things: ignorance and confidence.

Mark Twain

To laugh often and much, to win the respect of intelligent people and the affection of children, to leave the world a better place, to know even one life has breathed easier because you have lived—this is to have succeeded.

Ralph Waldo Emerson

On Challenges

"There are very few great men, only great challenges ordinary men are made to endure."

Admiral "Bull" Halsey,
Fleet Admiral, US Naval Forces in World War II

On Philosophy

"We are masters of our unsaid words, but slaves of those we let slip out."

Winston Churchill

Too often, we enjoy the comfort of opinion without the discomfort of thought."

John Fitzgerald Kennedy

Over the years I have used many such quotes in my lectures and presentations, but I think the one I favor most was written about the future of America and its democracy as seen through the eyes of a president in the midst of a very unpopular war:

"If destruction be our lot, then we ourselves must be its author and its executioner, for as a nation of free men, we are destined to live through all times, or die, by suicide." Abraham Lincoln

Using the wisdom and respect of those whom we know and admire will only enhance your presentation, and yourself along with it!

The Tenth Commandment of Communication
BREVITY

As a television Director, one of my objectives is to always leave audiences wanting more. After watching a two hour special I had done for The History Channel entitled *When Cowboys Were King,* a friend of mine, whom I've known since elementary school, called to discuss it with me and in the course of our conversation, he said, "I was really sorry to see it end." Without even realizing it, he had paid me the most sincere compliment of all—*I had left him wanting for more!*

Yet, when asked to speak before assemblies of people, your host may ask you to limit or prolong your talk to a specific length of time. We have already discussed how a thorough knowledge of your subject matter will allow you to do exactly that.

With that being said, however, remember the most persuasive arguments are *always* presented in the most succinct and brief manner.

Case in point:

One of history's best known, most revered, most quoted and most insightful speeches lasted only *two minutes,* but its greatness has been ordained to span the ages!

It was delivered by Abraham Lincoln on a battlefield in Gettysburg on a cold November morning in 1863.

I think Wikipedia defined it best when they wrote:

". . . In just over two minutes, Abraham Lincoln invoked the principles of human equality espoused by the Declaration of Independence and redefined the Civil War as a struggle not merely for the Union, but as 'a new birth of freedom' that would bring true equality to all of its citizens, create a unified nation in which states' rights were no longer dominant, defined democracy in terms of government of the people, by the people, for the people, and defined republicanism in terms of freedom, equality, and democracy."

To me, a great speech is like a good sermon: short, inspirational, succinct, and meaningful. Master those qualities and you will forever command both the attention and the respect of your audiences.

With that in mind, I will follow my own advice and end this chapter here!

Chapter Nine
LEADER OF THE PACK

The most effective form of embedded media is free media, and this chapter will teach you a step-by-step method to achieve just that, both locally and nationally!

As mentioned earlier, I began my media career in 1979.

As the new guy hanging around the news rooms, I remember some of the veteran reporters asking this riddle:

Question: *What does a reporter do on a slow news day?*

Answer: *You set up a camera and a microphone on any street corner in America and then cover the foot race between (a specific individual's name) and (the name of another, well-known individual) and then report on who gets in front of the camera first!*

Again, I think it prudent *not* to specifically identify the two individuals to whom my colleagues were referring—I'll let you guess that. But here's a hint, one's a male (initials JJ), the other's a female (initials GA); one hails from the legal profession, the other from politics and the pulpit.

One more hint, sadly, that old riddle and the two people to whom it refers, is still relevant today.

Whether you have guessed the two individuals involved or not is immaterial. What is material is the brilliance of their actions.

Think about it, the two individuals to whom this riddle refers have literally become household names, *worldwide*, but not for any personal prodigious achievement within their chosen field of expertise. They have become sought after news celebrity experts and self-appointed spokespersons for a wide range of individuals and causes for one reason and one reason only: *they are experts in using the news media to promote themselves and their causes!*

In essence, they have used media to appoint themselves leaders of their respective packs.

By following the techniques I've outlined in this book, and the ones I am about to disclose, you too can become the leader of *your* pack!

In Chapter Two, *Me, Myself and I,* I promised to teach you my proven methods of how to secure free and highly-effective airtime for you, your company, or your organization. So let's get to it.

Before discussing some up-to-date examples on how to succeed in obtaining that free media coverage in today's highly competitive media markets, I feel it important for you to fully understand the nuts and bolts as to how and why my method works as effectively today as it did when I first perfected it back in the late 1960s and 70s. To do that you must understand why the need arose in the first place.

It's been my experience that the clearest and easiest understood forms of examples are those based on fact, and since 1) controversial issues are often both the easiest and the most difficult circumstances to effectively exploit, and 2) since there are few things more controversial than an unpopular war, let's begin with The Vietnam War and how I obtained millions of dollars worth of on-air media in support of American Military Forces, their goals, objectives and programs in the midst of fighting that very unpopular and extremely controversial war.

However, remember, it makes very little difference what your topic, objectives, or credentials are, so long as your issue conforms to one or more the following criteria, namely, that it

1. Impacts the public at large;

2. Encourages your audience's hopes and dreams;

3. Improves the public's quality of life; or

4. Threatens the public's health or safety;

5. Excuses your audience's failures or shortcomings;

6. Makes, costs or saves the public money or

7. Impedes the public's needs, desires, or sense of comfort;

Or, finally,

8. By its very nature, it's controversial.

If your company, product, services, issues or philosophies apply to one or more of the aforementioned criteria, then these seven steps to obtain free media exposure will work just as effectively for you as they do for me.

Let's begin.

To reiterate, while serving as an Army Reservist, I was ordered to develop an effective method of seeking new recruits for the Reserves.

After some less than spectacular results at the local shopping center, I decided to take my message to both radio and television.

Remember, media exists to make money. To do that it must capture and hold audiences, and the best way to do that is to provide programming that has either a positive or negative impact on the health, safety, comfort, actions, needs, desires, interests or financial situations of those audiences.

TAILORING YOUR MESSAGE

Step One:

Tailor your message by determining how your presentation fits into one of those previously defined key categories.

In this case, I saw *two separate issues* upon which I could capitalize and through which media outlets would be able to provide programming interesting enough to capture and hold their audience's attention.

The first was job training.

At the time (the late 1970's), the nation was suffering from an unusually high rate of unemployment. Jobs were at a premium and those vocational schools offering to train people in new careers were very expensive.

However, within the ranks of the US Army Reserve, there were approximately 300 civilian-related jobs that ranged from cooks to truck drivers and from nurses to airplane mechanics; many of them very well paying in civilian life. Furthermore, not only was the job training free, but the Reserves would *pay you* to learn your new career! That factor alone could provide a much needed answer to those people seeking a profession rather than a job, but who lacked the money to pay for the needed training.

The second issue was the war itself which was *extremely* controversial and then, still going strong.

With those two issues, I felt confident I could offer media outlets subject matter that was both helpful and controversial and would appeal to large audiences, thus making their advertisers happy!

The first step is to carefully examine your media intent, i.e., the impact of your products or goals and objectives, institutions, policies etc. on the public at large, and then frame it in a way so that your message has a direct and definitive impact on your targeted media audiences.

SHOPPING THE MEDIA

Step Two:

Identify your media targets.

In the pre-internet era, the only way one could research potential media outlets was though laborious hours spent at your local Library.

Fortunately, today, thanks to the world of Cyber-Space, there are numerous resources to assist you in your search of any and all types of media entities. A friend of mine, Michael Mandaville, author of *Citizen Soldier Handbook,* told me about one sight which has categorized the nation's print media outlets by city, state and/or zip codes. You can find it at www.congress.org.

For a list of the nation's broadcast and cablecast outlets, I recommend www.stationindex.com/tv/.

For a list of the nation's radio stations, I have found www.radio-locator.com to be invaluable. As with the two previous sights, this site allows you to easily locate radio outlets by state, city or zip codes.

These three websites will provide you with the names and contact information of every known media outlet in the country.

Armed with access to that information, I then made a list of every broadcast media outlet within my targeted markets. Then I made a list of each of their broadcast formats (jazz, rock, classical, news, talk, etc.)

I recognized immediately, news or talk show formats would offer me greater opportunities for on-air interviews, debates and discussions so I concentrated on those formats first. (However, never rule out any media format because almost all of all of them offer information-oriented programming designated as community service.)

Step Three:
Identify the decision makers, i.e., guest bookers, of the targeted programs.

To do this, I contacted the program director of each of the selected stations and determined which of their talk or information-oriented programs were locally produced (i.e., produced in-house by that media outlet) and the on-staff person producing them.

Step Four:

Perfect your pitch.

As soon as I knew which talk / discussion oriented programs were produced at that particular station and who produced them, it was then time for me to develop a short, sweet and meaningful sales pitch. That pitch had to be just long enough to contain a few key words or concepts designed to capture the program producer's attention.

Once I perfected that, I'd call the different programs' producers and introduce myself using the most impressive credentials I could muster while still being honest.

It went something like this: *Hi (name of producer), I'm Staff Sergeant Michael S. Emerson, assigned to the Office of Chief of Army Reserve Operations at The Pentagon.*

To a program producer, the terms *Staff Sergeant* and *Pentagon* would usually grab their attention, at least for a moment or two. Within that window of opportunity, I would point out how unusually high unemployment rates were negatively affecting their audiences and then I'd ask if I could come on their program to discuss a unique career-training opportunity the Army Reserve was offering and how that program could be of interest and help to their audiences.

On a rare occasion, I'd get booked right then and there, but, most of the time, they'd ask me to send them a written request outlining my suggested topic.

Step Five:

Prepare your written request using the most impressive imagery and credentials possible.

In preparing my request, I'd made sure the stationery used was impressive enough to immediately catch and hold their attention at a glance. In this case, the heading read, The Department of the Army.

The letter was always less than a full page and written in paragraphs of no more than two or three sentences (tests have shown short paragraphs are more likely to be read and are easier to understand).

I would always reference our previous telephone conversation and then re state my case, i.e., current high unemployment; opportunity *for their audiences* to train for a career instead of just a job and the ability to be paid while being trained!

Step Six:

Be organized, polite, professional and persistent in your follow-ups.

I would always follow-up within 48 hours with a phone call to the program's producer and continue following up every few days until I received an answer. In each instance, I was respectful of their demanding schedules and always walked that thin line of being persistent without becoming a pest. Using this technique, my efforts proved successful in about two out of every five requests (or approximately 40% of the time).

If it were a television program, I'd end up either being interviewed on camera as a single guest, or as part of a discussion group, but in either case, I'd always appear in uniform as it served as a badge of authority and always commanded more attention. *Image!*

If it were a radio program, I'd be asked to be interviewed either in-studio, or via the telephone.

I was happy for the opportunity to participate in any manner possible, because it didn't matter wherever or whenever I appeared on a program, my message always became *part of the program itself* rather than a 30 or 60 second commercial spot scheduled to run at the break.

In today's terms, it is called embedded advertising and it is by far the most effective form of media campaigning.

When your message appears in the body of a program rather than as a commercial message positioned between the program's segments, several things occur:

1. Your discussion points immediately benefit from Media's Second Principle of Power: *The Imprimatur of Importance* (Chapter One). If what you're saying wasn't important, why would it be being discussed on the radio or television? And since it is important, your audience will pay closer attention to what you are saying;

2. When booked as part of a program's segment, your air-time should run anywhere from two minutes to thirty minutes, or more, with the average on-air interview segment lasting from seven to nine minutes. That's

a lot of time for you to make your points and state your case, and remember, depending on the program selected and the market in which it airs, you'll be making those points to an audience numbering from the tens of thousands into the millions.

Step Seven:

Know your material __and__ that of your adversaries.

Sound bytes are great for the six o'clock news, but a dialoged consisting only of short, inspiring statements will always come up shallow in the war of ideas.

Not only is it imperative that you familiarize yourself with every facet of every talking point in *your* argument, but it's also necessary for you to be able to articulate, dissect and then destroy the talking points of your detractors (or interviewers). It's an essential part of "Knowing Your Subject," and you never know when it will come in handy.

For me, it was while I was doing a live television program in San Francisco, California.

I had booked myself on the NBC O and O (owned and operated) television Station KNTV. The program was a morning talk show. When I arrived in uniform, the program's Host, an attractive, well informed and articulate news-style woman greeted me like a long lost friend. She explained how her husband was an Officer in the Naval Reserve and how she herself had come from a military family.

Remember, I was there to promote the 300 plus civilian-rated job training opportunities offered by the US Army Reserve to a city then gripped by double-digit unemployment.

Due to the complexities of the military and the different missions delegated to each of its branches, I always made it a point to suggest to my hosts / interviewers, should they ever draw a mental blank during the interview, simply ask me the question, "What is the difference between the Army Reserves and the National Guard?"

(This is a great technique to employ whatever your topic. Interviewers are human and they can easily lose their train of thought. If prior to your interview you offer them a trigger question they can ask you in case they run out of their own questions, it helps to put the interviewer at ease and that can make for a better interview.)

I explained that after answering that question, I'd move on to another topic from which they could then derive additional questions allowing the interview to continue uninterrupted.

Everything was going extremely well until the Stage Manager announced that we were live in 30 seconds. My interviewer and I exchange a few more pleasantries, and then as soon as the cameras went live, my hostess introduced me, told her audience why I was there, and then began the interview by asking, "*What can an organization whose job it is to kill people and destroy things possibly offer the people of San Francisco? Don't you think there is enough violence plaguing our streets already? Do you really think we need the military training our residents in the art of war?"*

I was dumbstruck, but only for micro-second.

I instantly understood that all her pleasantries were only designed to catch me off-guard and hopefully embarrass me, live, on camera.

However, because I was also cognizant of the unpopularity of the war, especially within the ranks of the media elite, I was prepared for her attack.

As I remember, I responded immediately and my answer went something like this;

"Although I am acutely aware of the reality that there is a war going on and over five hundred and fifty thousand of America's finest are engaged in it; what you may not realize is that only one in every thirteen soldiers ever carry a rifle. The rest of those brave people provide the supplies and logistics to those fighting units in the field people such as truck drivers, mechanics, hospital personnel, cooks, pilots, police and fire personnel, just to mention a few—and the United States Army Reserve can provide paid training in each of those fields, as well as some three hundred more, to any of your audience seeking an opportunity to learn a new, high paying, civilian-related profession in order to better their lives and those of their families".

I can still see her face with that blank stare on it.

There was a pregnant pause and then she asked me, *"What is the difference between the Reserves and the National Guard?"*

During the commercial breaks, she kept herself busy, never making eye contact with me nor engaging in any off-air conversations. The phone-in segments of the program proved to be positive, supportive and successful.

When the program finally ended some thirty minutes later and the Stage Manager called "Clear," she looked at me and said, "Sorry about that opening, I was just doing my job" and then walked off the set.

True story.

To be successful in using the media effectively, you need to be prepared *for anything, at anytime, under any circumstances.* To do so will only help ensure that your media efforts and appearances will work *for* you instead of *against* you.

For example, in 21st century America, there are numerous important, if not strategic industries, vital to the strength and well-being of our nation and her people, which are consistently and effectively subjected to on-going media attacks which result in the undermining of their effectiveness and public support.

Organizations such as America's Armed Forces; the nation's energy corporations; its pharmaceutical industries as well as its medical professionals just to name a few. That's not to say those industries and others like them don't deserve both scrutiny and occasional criticisms, but the bias with which they are reported on is a disservice to all involved, included the news organizations themselves, and here's why.

Thanks to this nation's media, especially the news media, the average American's perception of what these institutions (and others like them) do, why they do it and how they do it is so distorted, as to paint them as public enemies rather that some of our nation's greatest resources.

But I don't blame the news media for these misperceptions, I blame the industries and organizations themselves! If you've learned anything from this book, you've learned that the media is primarily driven by commercially-oriented forces (i.e., bad news is *great* news!).

Corporate America was conceived in competitive commercialism and it needs to use its knowledge of advertising and commercialism to re take the playing field by using the very media that attacks them to defend themselves, for their own sake, as well as those who benefit from their services, specifically, the public at large!

Remember, *People believe what they are told, not what they know* (more on that later). Consequently, if all the public ever hears are negative attacks and accusatory innuendos, that's what they will believe unless those being attacked step up to the plate, strike back and defend the truth!

Now back to the issues at hand: securing for yourself the most effective form of media penetration—embedded advertising—and doing it for free!

As previously mentioned, I have been using these techniques and advising others on how to use them for over three decades. That's why I know they work!

Remember, as long as your topic

1. Impacts the public at large;

2. Encourages your audience's hopes and dreams;

3. Improves the public's quality of life; or

4. Threatens the public's health or safety; or

5. Excuses your audience's failures or shortcomings;

6. Makes, costs or saves the public money, or

7. Impedes the public's needs, desires and/or sense of comfort;

or, finally,

8. By its very nature, it's controversial,

these same techniques will work for you. Case at hand:

While writing this chapter, I received a call from a new client seeking advice on how to get their product exposed on both local and national media.

Again, I don't think it appropriate to disclose their name, but I will tell you about their product. It's in the health services field.

They have developed an educational program for the caregivers (both professionals and family members) of those suffering an on-going and progressively debilitating Illness. One statistic they gave still haunts me, specifically, 50% of the caregivers themselves, will die before those for whom they are caring.

This statistic is due to the increased stress the caregivers themselves are made to endure as a result of the around the clock care-giving, supervision and services they provide their loved ones or patients.

Secondly, sadly, the specific illness being treated will afflict approximately three out of every ten adults, 60 years or older.

My client's primary interest is to reach *and help* as many of these targeted audiences as possible. Their secondary interest is to sell their perfected training techniques (via CDs, DVDs and books) to as many people as possible. Simple, clear, and concise.

Following my formula, their product or services apply to at least 3 of the 6 needed elements, specifically:

1. Impacts the public at large
2. Improves the public's quality of life; or
3. Threatens the public's health or safety;

I advised them as follows:

First:

In order to provide something appealing to a program's audiences, I suggested they create a short list of questions by which audiences could determine whether they or their loved ones were at risk of contracting this disease. (i.e. an issue that threatens their health or well being.)

Second:

For those in the audience whose loved ones were already afflicted with the disease, I suggested they create a list of three simple yet meaningful techniques they could share on camera or over the radio that would have a demonstratively positive impact on helping that caregiver administer their care.

Third:

I also asked them to be ready to share with their audiences a few ideas as to what those individuals suffering from the illness could do for themselves to better improve the quality of their life as well as those around them.

Easily done, they said.

Fourth

By freely providing, over the air, helpful techniques for both the caregiver as well those receiving the care *and* by adding information to determine whether or not they themselves or their own loved ones were at risk of contracting this disease, they had broadened their appeal to the widest possible media audience. Consequently, they now had something *both threatening, informative, and entertaining* to offer programming producers to help reach, capture and hold their audiences.

Now what about their product, i.e., the training program? What can they do to help facilitate the sale of those materials as part of their appearances?

I explained to them as part of their media appearances, while discussing the helpful information they were providing for free, they also needed to inform their audiences that additional free information and helpful tips were available to everyone through their website.

In other words, use every opportunity given them to drive their listening and viewing audiences to their website where, along side of the additional free information is, you guessed it, their complete training course is prominently displayed for all to see *and buy.*

Side Note: *To successfully drive as many people as possible to your website, your site's name must be simple to remember and even simpler to spell! Their website's address included a medical term which was hard to pronounce and impossible to spell. Consequently, I suggested they create a new, simpler and more memorable web address; one that audiences could easily remember and access.*

Why would you go to the trouble to inform, excite and motivate audiences to seek out your website if when they want to, they can't remember it or spell it correctly?

With those key elements now in place, they were ready to follow the seven steps outlined earlier in this chapter in order to book themselves on all the appropriate media formats.

However, there is another form of free media available to them—and you—that should also be discussed. It's called cable television. Allow me to explain.

The vast majority of the United States is wired for cable television and the majority of those systems have the right of "exclusivity of service" within their licensed areas. As part of their right to that exclusivity, many of them have had to stipulate to various public service conditions and one of those usually includes a commitment to provide what is commonly referred to as a public access channel which airs (actually cablecasts) within the confines of that community and its surrounding communities. (For instance, the system to which I subscribe services over a dozen local cities reaching several hundred thousand homes).

Going back to my client's scenario, as mentioned, they have a training course which I truly believe can and will improve the lives of those in need. They would like to expand that program into a ten part series of training classes, which they will in turn make available on DVD to both the public and medical services communities. However, that can become an expensive effort to produce those DVDs, unless of course, you follow another of my free media secrets.

Because their product actually helps individuals and families in need, if structured properly, they can actually use their local cable network production facilities to produce their DVDs for them! Here's how:

The major costs associated with the production of video/DVD programming fall into three primary areas: 1) research and development of the materials; 2) the actual video production (taping) of that material and, 3) the editing (post-production) of those produced materials.

What I suggested to my client was the following:

1. Break their training program into ten parts with each part addressing a single issue;

2. Structure each part as a 15 or 30 minute training segment;

3. Approach their local cable system and ask to produce their ten part series as part the cable system's Public Access channel programming.

Let me explain how this works. Each cable system will have their own criteria, but generally they will follow this line:

A. The programming must in the best interest of the public at large;

B. The programming cannot not be commercial in nature.

C. In return, the cable company will produce the program for them and they will do it for free!

That's right, they will do it for free because of their commitments to provide a public access channel as part of their exclusivity agreement.

Furthermore, my client will also be able to purchase a copy of each program for the cost of the video tape used, approximately twenty dollars ($20.00) per 30 minutes;

Let's recap.

First, by creating a program whose information will improve the quality of life for all those who may see it, said information is curtaining in the best interests of the public at large;

Second, by offering the information free any pretense of commercialism is removed, thus making it eligible for airing on Public Access; and

Third, once the program is produced, the program's creator can then can buy the *already produced and edited* program for as little as $20 to cover the approximate cost of 30 minutes of video tape!

Once you have the finished program (referred to as the edited master) if necessary, you can then use that edited master to re-edit into your ten part instruction training series into commercially viable DVDs for sales and marketing.

Furthermore, you will have accomplished that for a tiny fraction of what you would have had to pay if you were to try to produce and post it on your own!

Author's Note:

When it comes to getting yourself booked on or in various media outlets or publications, there are numerous individuals and companies ready to help you for a fee. (Just Google "How to get booked as a guest on media" and see for yourself). A word of caution however, be skeptical of their claims and always ask for real life references from people who have used and *benefited* from their services.

Remember, in the end, all these companies will be doing for you *for a fee* is what I have already taught you to do for yourself *for free!*

However, if you feel more comfortable having someone else promote you, then I suggest you start with those publications and/or groups who claim to be direct resource outlets for the working Media. Companies such as Radio-TV Interview Report (www.freepublicity.com); Reporter Connection (www.reporterconnection.com), and Great Guest Interviews (www.greatguestinterviews.com) just to name a few.

I do not personally know these companies and consequently cannot endorse them, so in the words of Ronald Reagan, before signing anything, always *trust but verify!*

EPILOGUE
MEDIA'S POWER TO PERSUADE
People believe what they are told, not what they know

Often, while lecturing, I will use a member of the audience to demonstrate the subliminal power of Media. After asking their permission, I will simply stand next to them, gently place my fingertip on their shoulder, and then continue on with my lecture. After a few minutes, invariably the impact of my finger becomes almost imperceptible to my volunteer.

Media works in almost the same manner.

In the same way your skin perceives the presence of clothes and then accepts that perception as normal or natural to the point of then dismissing or accepting that feeling without question, Media has come to permeate every aspect of our waking world to the point of where we have simply accepted it, and its influences, without questioning its validity nor its impact on our lives.

My purpose of writing *Mastering the Art of Media Messaging* was to demonstrate to those in Media's spotlight (and those who want to be) how it works, why it works, and then how to make it work for them.

Hopefully, I have accomplished that.

My last truism, which to me, personifies Media's power to "Mold the Minds of Modern Man," reads, *People believe what they are told, not what they know.*

On the surface, it sounds a little surreal, but sadly, in today's world, it's become all too real.

Author and media personality Dr. Phil McGraw, well-known for his ability to cut to the core of the issues frequently advises his audiences to simply "stick with what you know!" If more people did, Media would be forced to base their reports more on *facts* than *feelings* and rely more on their *intellect* than their *impressions*.

There are a plethora of statistics to substantiate the public's willingness to simply accept what they are told by media, rather than trusting their own instincts.

Here's just one example.

In the fall of 2007, a media related survey was released stating 53% of those surveyed believe the economy is in trouble. Nothing striking about that result. Until you look at the rest of the survey and realize that *82% of those 53% say financially, they are doing better than ever before.* How can that be? How can five out of ten people surveyed believe the economy was in trouble, when eight out of ten of those same people surveyed were doing better financially than ever before!

Maybe it was because of what the Media was reporting at that time.

In *early* November of 2007, The Consumer Federation of America sent out a press release stating, *35% of those surveyed reported, they were planning to spend less this upcoming Holiday season.* The timing of the story was of particular interest.

The day after Thanksgiving is considered to be the biggest shopping day of the year; Thanksgiving comes at the *end* of November.

For almost three weeks prior to the year's biggest shopping day, the national media repeatedly used this survey to report that *the upcoming Holiday shopping season was anticipated to be one of the worst in years.*

All major news organizations, when reporting on stories dealing with the economy and the upcoming holiday season, regularly grouped it (i.e., story association) with the survey released earlier by The Consumer Federation of America (remember, "bad news is *great* news"). The mere fact the story had been reported once gave it instant credibility by the media, but having it reported numerous times over several weeks elevated it to a much higher level of importance (the industry's term for this is "The story has legs"), thus making audiences accept it's validity almost without question. I.e., *53% of those surveyed believe the economy is in trouble.*

Of all the nationwide news agencies that reported the survey, only one reporter, that I know of, ever investigated The Consumer Federation of America, and then having done so, reported his findings to his audience. What that reporter found was, for each of the three previous years, the CFA had reported similar "surveys" and in each case, their predictions of a disappointing holiday shopping season were proven false!

Their record was zero for three!

That single reporter was Frank Mottek, the anchor for the KNX Business Hour which airs on the CBS owned and operated radio station located in Los Angeles, California. If that information was available to Mr. Mottek, it was certainly available to all of his news colleagues as well.

As a follow-up to that story, when the Thanksgiving figures for 2007's busiest shopping day of the year were finally reported, they showed *sales were up over 10 percent; the largest holiday sales increase in three years!*

If all of us would simply follow Dr. Phil's advice and "stick with what you know" and not what Media tells you, it would go a long way in holding Media accountable for its reporting (i.e., challenging their credibility) and thus leveling its playing field for the betterment of us all

Furthermore, the people participating in that reported survey had to know the Malls in which they were shopping were filled with people and that they themselves were most likely shopping and spending more (because, remember, *82% of those 53% said financially, they were doing better than ever before,* so why didn't they see through this obviously flawed report? Because . . . *People believe what they are told, not what they know.* Especially when they are told it by the Media!

In conclusion, I leave you with this final thought.

Recently, while listening to author, lecturer and nationally syndicated radio talk host, Dennis Prager (an individual whose insights on man's morality I always find thought-provoking), I heard him remark (and I'm paraphrasing), *"One of the failures of today's culture is its rush to bestow impor-*

tance on individuals whose contributions to our society lack significance, while denying importance to those individuals whose contributions are substantial."

When hearing it, I couldn't help but to think of it as another affirmation of Media's Second Principle of Power, *The Imprimatur of Importance,* i.e., *whomever or whatever Media focuses its attention is automatically bestowed the mantle of importance (thus fame), whether deserved or not.*

The bad news is, empirically speaking, you must always recognize that the consequence of having Media focus its attention on you, your organization, your events and issues will have as its ultimate result, either fame or infamy. That is why it is so important to take whatever steps possible to control the circumstances surrounding that exposure in order to ensure for yourself the most positive and effective consequences of that focus.

The good news is, *Mastering the Art of Media Messaging* has provided you step-by-step instructions on how to accomplish *exactly* that!

About the Author

If you're a fan of The History Channel, The Biography Channel, A&E or The Disney Channel, chances are, you're a fan of Michael Emerson as well.

Prior to completing work on the six-hour television min-series special for The History Channel entitled "Vietnam in HD," Michael completed work on History's historic award-winning, ten-part series "World War II in HD" and its follow up two hour special, "The Air War."

He has also directed and co-produced The History Channel's award-winning, two hour television specials, "When Cowboys Were King," "Hollywood's Greatest Villains," "70's Fever" as well as the A&E special, "Cecil B. De Mille" and "The James Woods Biography" among others.

Michael began his media career in 1979 with the creation and hosting of the radio feature "Face to Face," an issue-oriented, nationally syndicated radio news program that aired Monday through Friday, on 126 stations in the United States and 697 stations in 41 countries around the world. In 1984, after some 1,400 broadcasts, he left radio to expand his horizons in the fields of television and feature films.

Throughout his media career, he has been honored with nineteen national and international awards for his film and television achievements as well as winning two American

Political Consultant's coveted Polie Awards and was nominated for the Advertising Industry's prestigious Clio Award.

In addition to authoring the acclaimed books, *Mastering The Art of Media Marketing* and *The Ten Commandments of Communication,* his lifetime speaking and lecturing achievements have earned him an appointment as a visiting faculty member at the celebrated Leadership Institute in Washington, DC and a guest lecturer at the University of Southern California.

Michael is a member of The Academy of Television Arts & Sciences and currently heads up his own production and media relations company, Michael S. Emerson Productions, which specializes in the development and production of entertainment and advertising properties as well as the analysis of corporate and governmental media relationship programs.

In addition to his work as an author, producer and director, Michael also has a passion for public speaking and lectures extensively on Media and its impact on our lives.

Made in the USA
San Bernardino, CA
10 January 2015